Herbs and spices

A Hamlyn Colour Guide

Herbs and spices

by Jan Kybal

Illustrated by
Jiřina Kaplická

Hamlyn
London · New York · Sydney · Toronto

Translated by Olga Kuthanová
Graphic design by Aleš Krejča
Designed and produced by Artia for
The Hamlyn Publishing Group Limited
London · New York · Sydney · Toronto

ISBN 0 600 34613 7
Printed in Czechoslovakia
3/15/03/51-01

CONTENTS

WHAT ARE HERBS AND SPICES?

Music is perceived with the ear, fine art with the eye, but food is perceived by three senses — taste, smell and sight. This makes the culinary art a very exacting one, demanding the harmonious balance of all the various ingredients. Cookery is an art whereby raw materials, both animal and vegetable, are transformed into tasty dishes. And it is herbs and spices that give these the flavour and piquancy that distinguishes the fare of the various nations historically, culturally and geographically. It is herbs and spices that give food flavour, aroma and often also colour.

When Alcuin, famous early medieval scholar and adviser to Charlemagne, asked his sovereign what a herb is he received the succinct reply: 'Friend of physicians and pride of cooks'. How much more apt and explicit is this old and perhaps apocryphal statement than all the contemporary definitions by renowned experts attempting to describe herbs and spices in the exact terms of modern science. We must also, however, accept the authoritative word of modern encyclopedias which state that herbs and spices are the fresh, dried or otherwise prepared parts of various plants with distinctive flavours and aromas used to season food.

BOTANIC CLASSIFICATION

The plant kingdom is divided by botanists into categories called taxons. On the basis of their mutual relationship plants are divided into phyla, classes, orders and families in that order (these basic taxons are often divided further into subgroups). The family to which a plant belongs is a very important category in the classification of plants (this name appears in the heading of the text accompanying each colour plate). It is broad enough to denote all the characteristic traits of the plants it embraces and at the same time narrow enough to state all that is essential. It is noteworthy that one often encounters the names of the same families in the case of plants used as herbs and spices. That is because the related plant species and genera, besides having similar morphological characteristics such as the shape of the flower, inflorescence and type of fruit, also exhibit similarities in the chemicals they produce and store in their tissues; in the case of herbs and spices, flavouring and aromatic substances.

Every plant has a scientific, Latinized name composed of two words. The first denotes the name of the genus to which it belongs and the second the species. Every plant family takes its name from the generic name of one of its members. Thus, for example, all species of the genus *Allium* (onion, garlic, chives, leek) belong to the Liliaceae family because their

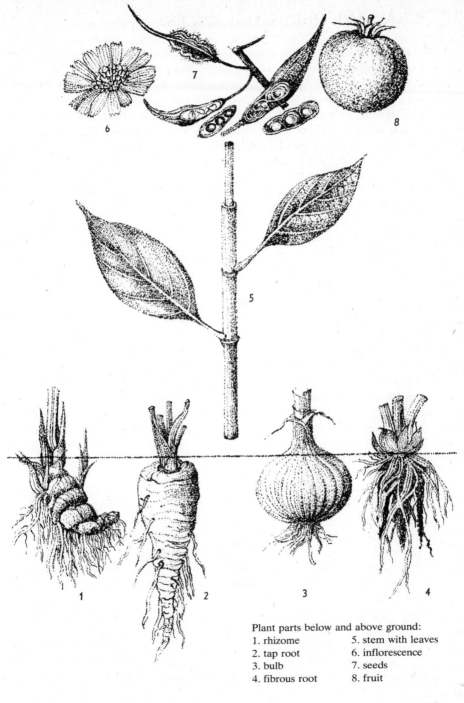

Plant parts below and above ground:
1. rhizome
2. tap root
3. bulb
4. fibrous root
5. stem with leaves
6. inflorescence
7. seeds
8. fruit

7

basic characteristics are similar to those of lilies (genus *Lilium*); thyme, sage, rosemary, oregano, basil, peppermint, balm, marjoram and hyssop, together with dead-nettle (genus *Lamium*), to the Lamiaceae family; clove and allspice are related to myrtle (Myrtaceae family); turmeric and cardamom to ginger (Zingiberaceae family), and so on.

The smallest and lowest taxonomic unit, designating very closely related plants of the same species, is the subspecies, sometimes also called variety. Garden forms bred and cultivated by man to better meet his needs, but not found growing in the wild, are called cultivars.

Spicy and aromatic substances are not present in all parts of the plant, as a rule, but only in certain organs. Most higher plants consist of an underground part (root, sometimes a bulb or rhizome) and green top parts (stem and leaves). Flowers are modified leaves and are usually arranged in inflorescences varying in arrangement. Following fertilization these develop into fruits containing seeds. In herbs the term herbage refers to the green non-woody stems and foliage and the term bark to the outside covering of the woody stem (branch).

AROMA AND FLAVOUR

Most herbs and spices are native either to the sunny Mediterranean region or the hothouse environment of the tropics: in other words ideal regions with plenty of light, heat and atmospheric moisture. These 'pampering' conditions cause the plants to produce excess quantities of primary metabolites (substances used to build all the plant organs), as well as secondary metabolites (substances that are not essential to their existence and without which the plants can function quite normally). Among the latter also belong various aromatic, flavouring or colouring substances which make the spices what they are. These secondary metabolites are very diverse, and often distinguished by a pronounced aroma and flavour as well as important pharmacological properties. That is why many herbs used in cooking are also used in medicine. Typical substances found in herbs are first and foremost essential oils, bitter principles and tannins.

Essential or volatile oils are accumulated by plants in special cells. These are visible even with the unaided eye. For example, on a leaf held up to the light they are readily apparent as translucent spots and on fresh lemon peel they form slight elevations which burst, ejecting fragrant volatile oils, when crushed. These special cells are ideal containers which serve to protect the plant's 'perfume' from decomposing and evaporating. All volatile oils have a specific aroma and are liquid and vaporize quickly at low temperatures. They are insoluble in water but dissolve very readily in fats. Volatile oils differ widely in chemical composition. There are some

3,000 known essential oils and to date scientists have isolated and determined the chemical structure of more than 1,000 substances they contain. Those plant families which provide us with our kitchen herbs and spices (Rutaceae, Lauraceae, Lamiaceae, and Daucaceae) are particularly noted for their high content of essential oils.

Besides essential oils, many herbs contain so-called garlic oils. These are the seasoning element of all members of the genus *Allium* and their characteristics are similar to those of essential oils. However, an additional distinctive trait is that they occur in the plant in bound form releasing neither flavour nor aroma. That is why onion and garlic can be stored in the pantry together with other foods without any danger of their being contaminated by the characteristic pungent odour. This is emitted by the plant only when its tissues are bruised (when they are sliced, diced or crushed), which releases an enzyme that causes the decomposition of the garlic oils accompanied by a pungent odour. The same is true of the so-called mustard oils present in herbs of the Brassicaceae family, e. g. in the seeds of mustard, leaves of garden cress, and roots of horseradish.

Another important group of substances found in some herbs (wormwood, hops, chicory) are the so-called bitter principles. These are substances of varied chemical composition but with one characteristic in common − their strong bitter taste. Bitter herbs are also effective in aiding digestion as they promote the flow of digestive juices.

The pleasant astringent taste of other herbs (nettle, rose hip) is caused by the presence of tannins. Unlike essential oils, bitter principles and tannins are soluble in water and do not vaporize when heated.

A HISTORY OF HERBS AND SPICES

Next to touch, taste and smell are the oldest and most developed senses in the entire animal kingdom and it is not surprising that in the course of evolution the diet of the various animal species became specialized (limited to one type of food). Such a diet, however, is a great handicap if the food happens to be in short supply. Man solved the problem by gradually learning to prepare edible dishes from practically all the organic matter available on this earth.

Man's oldest ancestors fed on the seeds of grasses, although later they began to occasionally eat the flesh of various animals. This was eaten raw for fire was unknown to them and so they had no knowledge of cooking. The change to the present wide assortment of foods took place slowly and our day and age continues to see an increase in the variety of foods, which is mainly due to the use of herbs and spices. Thanks to these it is possible to make a tasty pâté even from seaweed.

In the beginning herbs and spices provided a welcome variety to man's diet; later they became a cultural custom, and finally a necessity. India provides us with a graphic example of this development. In about 2,000 B.C., rice was practically the sole food of the poor population of India's Malabar Coast. This region, however, was also the cradle of tropical herbs and so the natives soon learned to mix pepper, cardamom, ginger, turmeric and coconut milk to make a yellow paste that gave the bland rice a piquant flavour. This mixture became the basis of the curry-powder we use today.

References to herbs and their use may be found in Chinese documents from as far back as 3,000 B.C. Ancient Egyptian recipes on papyrus from the middle of the second millenium B.C. called for the use of herbs such as anise, mustard, caraway, coriander, mint, wormwood, cinnamon and saffron. The cuneiform inscriptions on clay tablets prove that the Sumerians cultivated fennel, caraway, coriander, saffron and thyme in Mesopotamia and that way back in ancient times the Indians were already acquainted with the use of cardamom, turmeric, cloves, nutmeg, pepper and cinnamon. There exist many records from the days of ancient Greece, thanks to the great physician Hippocrates and the Greek philosopher Theophrastus, as well as from the days of the Roman Empire, thanks to

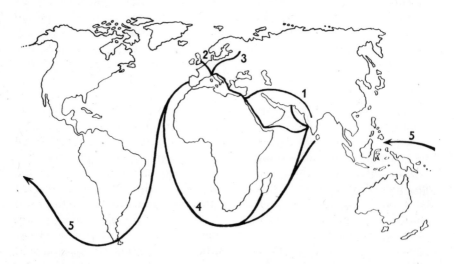

Map showing the original distribution of herbs and spices
Routes of the herb and spice trade
1. Military campaigns of Alexander the Great 327 B.C.
2.−3. Trade routes in Europe
4. Voyage of Vasco da Gama
5. Magellan's voyage

the Roman scholar Pliny. As we see, herbs were used by man long before the advent of modern civilization.

At first the various herbs and spices were known and used only in those places where they grew naturally in the wild. This applies not only to the tropical species from the Malabar Coast, but also to the aromatic herbs of the Mediterranean region as well as to the vanilla and red pepper of America. That is why in the days when there was still no means of communication between these distant lands we see the emergence of distinctive native dishes that have remained characteristic for the given region to this day, even though the local cuisine is becoming increasingly more cosmopolitan with the spread of civilization.

The herbs and spices of the Mediterranean region owe their spread throughout Europe chiefly to Charlemagne who recognized their importance in cooking during his many military campaigns. In the year 812 he included in the instructions to the steward of the royal household a list of 74 herbs which he ordered to be grown in the imperial gardens. This list has survived as part of his famous manuscript *Capitulare de villis* and includes the following: fenugreek, sage, cumin, rosemary, caraway, tarragon, anise, mint, parsley, celery, onion, chives, lovage, dill, fennel, savory and black mustard.

The late Middle Ages might be called the Golden Age of Herbs and Spices for that period saw the emergence of the science of cookery and housekeeping; the period that gave us our first cookbooks. Cookery was considered an art and a properly prepared dish the best of medicines. The following recipe for 'Douce Ame' (meaning 'sweet breath'), recorded in 1390 by the head cook at the court of Richard II of England, is an example of the recipes of that day.

Translated from the old English it reads: 'Take good cow's milk and pour it in a pot. Take parsley, sage, hyssop, savory and other good herbs, add them to the milk and boil. Take roast capons, cut them into small pieces, and add strained honey. Add salt, saffron for colour, and serve.'

The importance ascribed to cookery in those days is testified to by the fact that the cookbook from which the above recipe is taken was written 'with the approval of the council of physicians and scholars at the royal court'. It was published in London in 1780 under the title *Form of Cury* (meaning cookery). Among other things, it explains how to prepare roast peacock, fried apple blossom patties, herb salad, Hippocrates' wine and other medieval delicacies from the royal kitchens. Less aristocratic is the medieval French book *Le Ménagier de Paris* published in 1393, which, besides numerous recipes, also includes instructions on how to grow hyssop, fennel, savory, rosemary, marjoram and other kitchen herbs.

Tropical spices made their way to Europe by a far more complicated route. The Vedas, ancient sacred books of Hinduism written in Sanskrit during the 16th to 9th century B.C., contain the first mention of pepper. Hence, in all probability, it was used by the Indians long before that. In the first millenium B.C., the Indians made their way as far as the Persian Gulf and Red Sea, introducing pepper to the cultured nations of the Orient, mainly the Persians. Of the Europeans, the first to be introduced to pepper were the Greeks, who during the military campaigns of Alexander the Great got as far as India in 327 B.C.

It was not long before the Romans learned about pepper from the Greeks and began to trade with India through the intermediary of the South Arabians (Yemenites). By the second century A.D., the Romans were no longer trading through an intermediary. Their ships sailed from Alexandria along the southeastern canal built by the Egyptian pharaohs not only to the Arabian reloading site Arabia Felix, but also as far as India. Because of its geographical location Alexandria served as the main storage center for the precious herbs and spices, chiefly pepper, cinnamon and ginger, and it was there that the Romans collected duty on the imported goods. Because of their high price, trade in herbs and spices was engaged in only by the privileged and high-ranking families of Greece and Rome.

The siege and conquest of Rome by the Visigoth king Alaric at the beginning of the 5th century was the means whereby pepper was introduced to the Germanic peoples, with whom it rapidly became popular.

The end of the Crusades, which from the end of the 11th to the end of the 13th century took Europe's Christians to the lands of the eastern Mediterranean, saw the marked spread of trade in herbs and spices. Many politically independent Italian states had taken part in the Crusades and these tried to gain a monopoly of trade with the Orient. The city-state of Venice was the most successful and soon became the largest medieval city in the world (population 200,000), due to its trade in spices, silk and oils. Herbs and spices were then shipped from Venice to the other parts of Europe — across Brenner Pass, from Innsbruck to Basel, and along the Rhine to the North Sea and to England. Such a tortuous route naturally further raised the price of the already costly goods. The other route branched off at Innsbruck and led through Augsburg on to Nuremberg and Leipzig, to the trade centres of the Baltic Sea and as far as the old Russian commercial centre, the Boyar republic of Novgorod.

Venice had a monopoly on the profitable trade in herbs and spices until the conquest of Constantinople by the Turks in 1453 which thus blocked the route to India. This resulted in the gradual decline of Venice's power, though the cost of herbs and spices continued to rise.

Desire for the riches from eastern and southern Asia reached new heights following the publication of the book by Marco Polo, who had travelled extensively through China for 17 years and was the first European to see Indian pepper growing in its native habitat. The book, written in 1298, was soon translated into many languages and became a medieval bestseller. Its greatest importance rests in the fact that it inspired the voyages of Christopher Columbus and Vasco da Gama which led not only to the discovery of a direct sea route to the East Indies, but also to the chance discovery of America. 'Chance' in that, as everyone knows, Columbus did not set out to discover a new continent but a new route to India, the land of herbs and spices.

The efforts of Vasco da Gama, the Portuguese navigator, met with greater success when he sailed from Europe round the Cape of Good Hope to the Malabar Coast in 1498, returning to Lisbon with a rich cargo of herbs and spices. On a second voyage in 1502 he reached Ceylon. In 1524 he was appointed viceroy of India for his discoveries, which enriched Portugal and raised her to the front rank among European nations. In time Portugal had a monopoly on the lucrative trade in herbs and spices, supplying Europe with pepper, cinnamon, nutmeg and ginger. The Mediterranean remained relatively unimportant as a trade route until the opening of the Suez Canal and Venice was replaced by Lisbon as the centre of commerce in herbs and spices.

Portugal's influence was extended later as far as Madagascar, Sumatra and Java, and above all to Malacca, famed spice port in the south Malay Peninsula. The island of Ternate became the centre of the spice trade and despite the persistent and often bloody defense of the native Muslims the Portuguese gradually gained a monopoly on the world spice trade.

Portugal's greatest competitors at that time were the Spaniards, who sought a shorter route to India, one that would not entail sailing round the southernmost tip of Africa. As chance would have it it was again a Portuguese — Fernão de Magalhães, better known as Magellan, who in the service of Spain and financed by the Spanish King Carlos V, sailed westward in 1519 with a crew of 265 and discovered a new route. In 1521 he discovered the Philippine Islands where he was killed in a skirmish with the natives. Only a single ship from the entire flotilla reached the Moluccan island of Tidor to return home after three years with the surviving 18 members of the crew and a cargo of cloves. Their commander. Juan Sebastian del Cano, was raised to the ranks of the nobility and assigned 12 cloves, 3 nutmegs and 2 cinnamon sticks to his coat-of-arms. The imminent competitive struggle between the Spaniards and Portuguese was forestalled by marriages between the two ruling houses and by Carlos V selling his spice islands to his brother-in-law Juan III for 350,000 ducats.

Portugal's monopoly lasted until the end of the 16th century when the Dutch freed themselves from Spanish rule and founded a powerful, independent and flourishing state in the northern Low Countries. The first

13

Dutch expedition reached the spice islands in 1595. Before long the Dutch established good trade relations with the local sultans and took over the whole monopoly, with Amsterdam becoming the centre of the spice trade.

Holland's success prompted the foundation of the English East India Company by London merchants in 1600, to which the Dutch retaliated two years later by founding the Dutch East India Company in 1602. From then on there was stiff competition between the two with each fighting for control of the spice trade. One happy outcome, however, was that Europe came to know not only Oriental spices but also silk and porcelain.

Spices thus indirectly led to a flourishing trade with the Orient and a heightened interest in the exotic, which was one of the most marked elements of European culture in the 17th and 18th century. An important role was played by the East India Companies which had a monopoly on trade with southern and southeast Asia. This laid the foundation for English colonial rule in India and Dutch rule in Indonesia. The colonizers tried to preserve their monopoly by stringent measures designed to prevent the cultivation of spices on territory belonging to other nations but in this they were successful only for a time. In the course of the 18th century the cultivation of herbs and spices spread throughout the tropics.

Exotic herbs and spices also became fashionable at the courts of Europe in the 17th and 18th century (particularly at the court of Louis XIV) and the new class of wealthy merchants in Holland and in the free towns of the Hanseatic League made liberal use of herbs and spices at their lavish feasts. This is reflected in the still-lifes by the Dutch painters of that period. The sobriety of the early 19th century, marked by a preference for Biedermeier sweets eaten while sipping coffee or chocolate, was replaced at the end of the century by a newly revived interest in the cookery of distant lands. Chinese, Indian, Indonesian and other restaurants sprang up in Paris, London and other major European cities and have remained popular and successful to this day.

Herbs and spices have been gaining in popularity since the end of World War II — not only in restaurants but also in the household. Skilful use of herbs and spices is important in all good cookery. It is becoming a hobby for many people not only to cook with herbs and spices, but also to be able to identify fresh herbs, grow them at home or in the garden, and preserve them for winter use.

COLOUR ILLUSTRATIONS

Calamus, Sweet-flag
Acorus calamus

Calamus is a perennial herb up to 150 cm (5 ft) high, native in all probability to the Himalayas. It was known to Indian physicians in ancient times and was brought to Europe, to the Greeks and Romans, by Arabian and Phoenician merchants. The plant was discovered in India by the troops of Alexander the Great during one of his military expeditions. The first dried specimen in central Europe was obtained by the Italian physician Mattioli from the German ambassador to the court of Constantinople in the 16th century. Shortly after, the botanist Clusius cultivated the first rhizomes at the Vienna botanical garden which he propagated and sent to many other botanical gardens. From then on calamus spread rapidly and nowadays it grows wild throughout Europe, including the British Isles, as well as in the Atlantic region of North America. It grows by the edges of ponds, slow-moving water courses, in moist ditches and marshes.

The dried and ground rhizomes are a traditional seasoning in the sweet dishes and fruit compotes of the Indian and Islamic cuisine. In England and America calamus was at one time candied. The tender young leaf shoots make a very good salad that stimulates the appetite. Its main use, however, is in the preparation of liqueurs that aid digestion.

2

Calamus has creeping rhizomes that are 3 cm (1 in) thick, reach a length of 50 cm (20 in) and have numerous roots on the underside (1). The flowers (2) are arranged in a sessile, cylindrical spadix. After removing the roots, the rhizome is dried at room temperature either whole, or halved lengthwise and peeled. It has a pleasant pungent odour and bitter taste. Calamus may also be grown by the home gardener, most successfully in a natural situation. The plants are readily propagated by cutting up the rhizomes into 5- to 10-cm- (2- to 4-in-) long pieces and planting at a depth of about 10 cm (4 in). The best-quality seasoning is obtained from the rhizomes of two- to three-year-old plants.

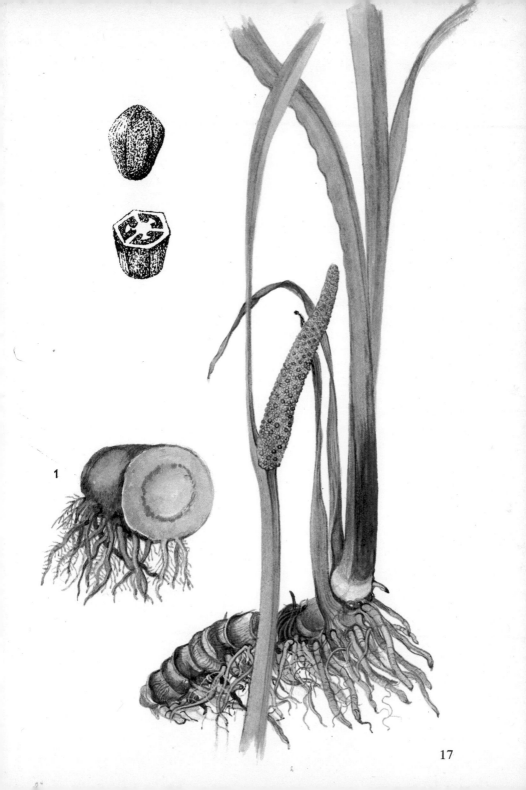

Meadow Mushroom, Champignon

Agaricaceae

Agaricus bisporus

The meadow mushroom, or champignon, is the first edible mushroom to be cultivated by man, and it soon became a lucrative product first on a small and later on a large, industrial scale. Credit for this goes to the 17th-century French botanist Marchant and the Parisian nurserymen of that day who grew melons in frames based on horse manure. Such an environment is also perfect for mushrooms; not only for the growth of mycelium but also for the development of the fruiting bodies. The first mushrooms harvested from these frames developed from chance spores carried there by the wind from neighbouring fields. The frames were covered for the winter to retain the heat generated by the gradual decomposition of the horse manure and the mushrooms were harvested successively throughout the winter. When Marchant succeeded in discovering how mushrooms multiplied, their cultivation no longer needed to be left to chance. Nowadays, when mushrooms are becoming increasingly scarce in fields and meadows because of the spread of intensive farming, fully mechanized, large-scale mushroom-growing plants provide many more times the amount than could be collected in the wild.

Mushrooms are not only a popular food that is low in calories, but also a delicate seasoning for soups, omelettes, meats and sauces. Young meadow mushrooms may be pickled and used in salads or served with roast meat, sausages or salami.

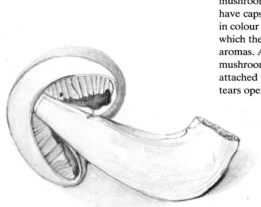

There are several kinds of meadow mushrooms that vary in appearance. They have caps that are smooth or scaly and range in colour from white to brown, besides which they also have different flavours and aromas. A characteristic feature of young mushrooms is a convex cap closed by a veil attached to the stalk or stipe; the veil later tears open, leaving a distinct ring on the

stipe (1). The gills on the underside of the cap are pale pink at first, later turning brown to black. Fully ripe mushrooms with spreading caps are the most flavoursome, as a rule. As fresh meadow mushrooms are available in shops throughout the year there is no need to dry them for use in the kitchen.

Common Onion

Allium cepa

Onion cooked in salt water was the chief food of the poorest peoples of central Asia, Asia Minor and the Mediterranean region in days of old. It was also the mainstay of the diet of Egyptian labourers, who built the ancient pyramids in the third millenium B.C. Having been cultivated for thousands of years, it is a plant whose land of origin remains unknown. The only onion with which we are acquainted is that found in cultivation or growing naturalized in the wild. We do know, however, that it was already cultivated by the Sumerians in 4,000 B.C. It was perhaps developed by breeding and selection from the wild species *Allium oschaninii* of central Asia, which was introduced to Europe by the Greeks and Romans.

A common, cheap and readily available food, the onion has become widely used as seasoning in many dishes, to which it gives an appetizing flavour and aroma. Nowadays we tend to be unaware that it is the most widely used of all herbs. Finely chopped raw onion is used in preparing steak tartare, and lightly sautéed in butter or oil it enhances the flavour of most soups and sauces as well as braised meat. It is the principal ingredient of the vegetable relish known as mixed pickles. The onion's metamorphosis from a vegetable into a seasoning is also apparent in recent years by its being available at shops in dried, finely-sliced form. This is used in the same way as fresh onion and is suitable for frying.

Onion is a biennial that stores food in a bulb the first year and flowers the following year. The leaves and flowering stem are hollow. The large globose flower head — an umbel — is composed of numerous, greenish-white flowers on long stalks.

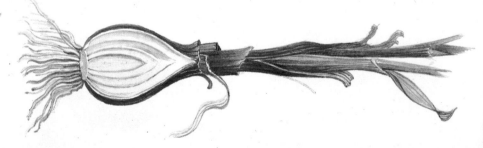

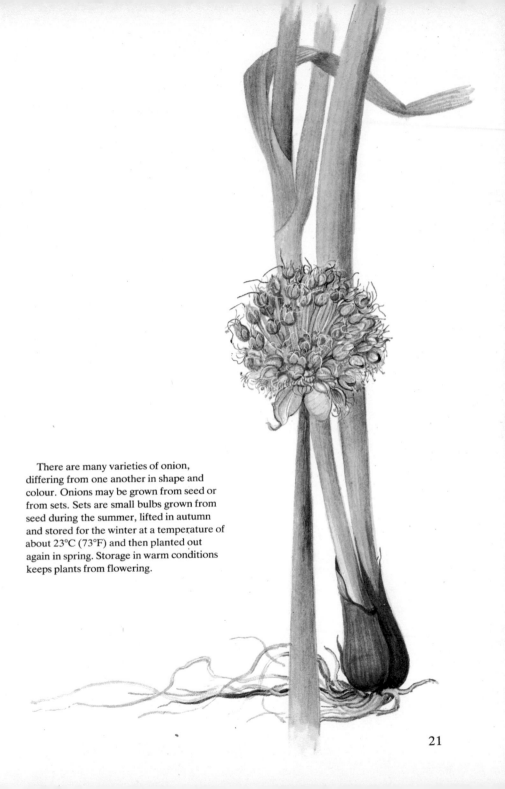

There are many varieties of onion,
differing from one another in shape and
colour. Onions may be grown from seed or
from sets. Sets are small bulbs grown from
seed during the summer, lifted in autumn
and stored for the winter at a temperature of
about 23°C (73°F) and then planted out
again in spring. Storage in warm conditions
keeps plants from flowering.

Shallot
Allium ascalonicum

Liliaceae

Like the onion, the shallot was also cultivated in central Asia and Asia Minor in olden times. Its name — *Allium ascalonicum* or onion of Ascalon — is derived from the town of the same name in Palestine where it was most widely grown and whence it was introduced to Europe by the Crusaders.

Shallot, as well as other kinds of onion and garlic, was a popular food of the Jews. In the second century A.D., when the Roman emperor Marcus Aurelius came to Palestine, after having conquered the Marcommani, the Quadi (both Germanic tribes) and the Sarmatians (an ancient Indo-Iranian people) during his military campaign in Egypt, he found the stench of the onion- and garlic-eating Jews so offensive that he cried out: 'Oh Marcommani, Quadi and Sarmatians, I have finally found a people that are even worse than you!'

Onions are composed mainly of water (about 88%). The substance that has a biting quality and causes the eyes to water when slicing onions is fructane, a volatile oil containing allylsulphides. It is these that class onions as kitchen herbs. Onions are also an important source of Vitamin C and B, some Vitamin A, and substances known as phytoncides (substances with excellent germicidal effects found in higher plants, e. g. allin in garlic, tomatin in tomatoes and lupulone in hops.)

Shallot usually has a more pungent flavour than common onion and is widely used in French, American and Russian cookery. It does not, as a rule, bear fruits, usually forming small sessile bulbils on the flower stalk the same as garlic. The obliquely-ovate bulbs form clusters, with one resting on top of the other. Each is composed of further tiny bulbs arranged in tightly compressed pairs. The bulbs are covered with several reddish skins. Shallot is generally propagated from small individual bulbs, though some forms produce viable seeds which are sown in spring.

23

Fistulosum or Welsh Onion

Allium fistulosum

The cross-section of a bulb of this onion reveals that it is composed of thickened, fleshy leaf bases tightly wrapped around each other. The outermost skin gives the bulb its colour, which varies, depending on the variety, from silvery white, white to dark brown, red and violet. It also protects the bulb from drying out and therefore should not be removed during storage.

The Welsh onion has a milder flavour than the common onion. Unlike the latter, which is grown as a biennial, it is hardy and perennial. Another advantage is that the small elongated bulbs grow in clusters as part of one single bulb which breaks up into several smaller onions as it grows. The Welsh onion has a swollen flowering stem growing up to 2 cm (3/4 in) thick and 30 to 60 cm (1 to 2 ft) tall. Being a native of southeastern Siberia it is resistant to frost and will overwinter successfully outdoors. The green parts may be used the same as chives.

Even though it had been grown in China two thousand years ago the Welsh onion was not known in medieval Europe until the 16th century when it was introduced via Russia. Nowadays it is cultivated in both Europe and America. Its requirements are light to medium, weed-free soil that is not too moist and an open, sunny position. The soil must not be freshly fertilized but it must have sufficient humus and lime present. As in other onions, the irritant action is produced by an essential oil containing organically bound sulphur.

Onion was considered a sacred plant at one time and used by the Persians, Jews and Egyptians in their religious ceremonies.

Leek

Allium porrum

Today's cultivated varieties of leek are derived from the species *Allium ampeloprasum* which grows wild in the Mediterranean region, as well as in southern England and Persia. It was cultivated by the ancient Egyptians, Greeks and Romans and is also mentioned in the Old Testament. It was so popular with the Romans that they even had a special name — 'porrinae' — for gardens where it was grown. In present-day England and America the leek is usually used only as a vegetable, whereas in Europe, particularly in France, it is also used as a kitchen herb.

The leek is a biennial herb, but is treated as an annual, because in the second year it flowers and dies. It need not be dug up in autumn for, as a rule, it is not damaged by frost and so can be taken fresh from the garden any time of the year. This is a great advantage, for although fresh leek tastes like the mildest of onions, it acquires an unpleasant strong taste when stored.

The leek is used primarily as a seasoning for vegetable soups and other vegetables. It is also used in preparing fish soup, cooking fish and crabs, as well as in pork and lamb dishes.

Planting the seedlings in deep holes and earthing-up the plants blanches the leeks. The blanched sections are much more tender than the green parts, which are usually discarded.

Even though many different (often regional) forms are grown and sold throughout the world, leeks can be divided into two basic groups. Large, plump leeks (1), which also give large yields, are used as a vegetable, whereas the smaller slender leeks (2), are recommended for use as a culinary herb. Those who find onion too pungent for their taste can use leek instead. The Romans even used young leeks to make a salad.

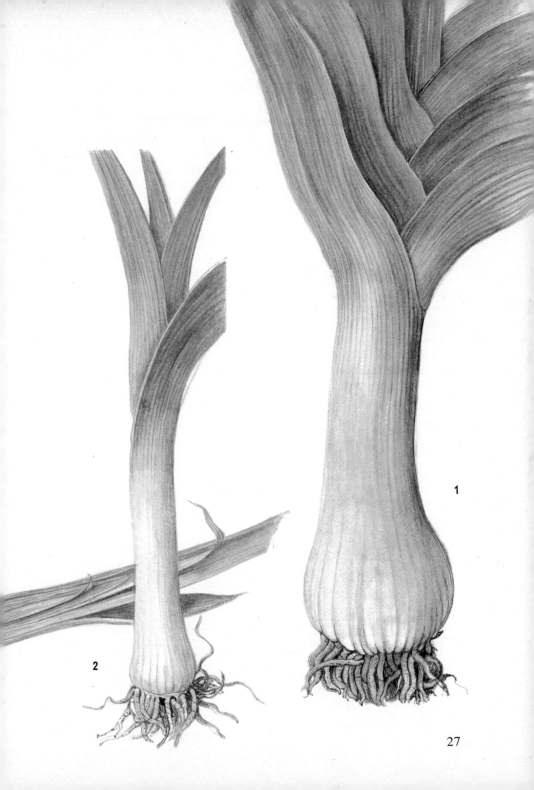

1

2

27

Garlic
Allium sativum

Liliaceae

Garlic is native to the steppes of the Djungar and Kirghiz region of central Asia, from where the Mongols soon introduced it to China. As we learn from Herodotus's writings it was also cultivated on a large scale in ancient Egypt. Garlic was even considered to be a sacred plant and ancient Greeks and Romans, believing it to have invigorating properties, fed it to their armies during military campaigns. Patricians, however, disdained garlic, giving it instead to their slaves. Since time immemorial garlic has been a favourite food of the Jews. As the Old Testament tells us the Jews cried to Moses: 'We remember the fish, which we did eat in Egypt freely... and the leeks and onions and garlic'.

Nowadays garlic is widely used as seasoning throughout the world, but it is used most by the peoples of southern Europe, north Africa and South America. It plays an important role in lands noted for their excellent cuisine, from France to China. Its uses are many: crushed together with salt in green salads; as seasoning for sauces, vegetables and meat dishes (beef and mutton), sausages and salamis, and fish. Besides being a seasoning it also has many important medicinal properties; it prevents flatulence and destroys intestinal parasites, checks the growth of bacteria, and is used in the treatment of arteriosclerosis. The chief exporting countries are USA (California), Egypt, Bulgaria, Hungary and Taiwan.

The bulb is made up of large segments called cloves (1) encased in a cover of scales ranging in colour from white to red. Unlike the common onion, the bulb of garlic is not made up of layers and the leaves are not hollow and tubular but flat. The flowers are arranged in loose umbels and are followed by small bulbils (2,3). Garlic is a perennial

herb propagated by planting the separate
cloves directly in the ground where they are
to grow, either in autumn or early spring.
Bulbs are dug up and harvested when the
foliage begins to turn yellow and dry. A very
suitable and decorative method of storing
garlic is to braid the bulbs together and hang
them up in a cool spot. Until recently the
housewife used either fresh or dry garlic
bulbs, but nowadays, thanks to modern
methods of dehydration, it can be obtained
in shops in the form of dry pieces, flakes,
grains or powder, all of equally good quality.

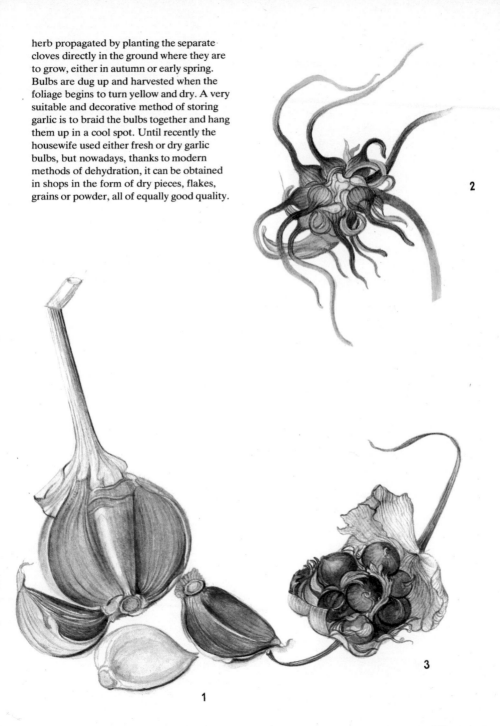

2

1

3

Chives
Allium schoenoprasum

If we were given a choice of growing only one species from the large genus *Allium* the decision would be very difficult, but many persons would doubtless choose chives. Chives can be easily grown, not only in the garden but also in a windowbox or in a pot on the window sill. They are frost-resistant and their leaves may be snipped the whole year long without affecting the plants in any way. However, they should be fed frequently and should not be cut too close to the ground so as to avoid damaging the growth centres. Chives may be propagated from seed, but home-growers usually increase them by splitting up older clumps and replanting the offsets, which gives earlier yields. The only requirement is plenty of light. Chives should be freshly cut before serving. They have a very mild onion flavour without the biting quality and are used not only as a herb but also as a garnish on many cold and hot dishes. They should never be cooked — when used as a garnish for hot dishes chives should be sprinkled on top just before serving. They are popular in cheese spreads, on bread and butter, in scrambled eggs, salad dressings and cold sauces, sprinkled on buttered boiled potatoes and as a garnish for assorted cold meat platters. In winter they are a welcome source of Vitamin C.

The fact that chives have no special growing requirements is testified to by their widespread distribution throughout the world. They grow wild in Europe and Asia (even in Siberia and Kamchatka) as well as in North America, mainly round the

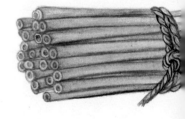

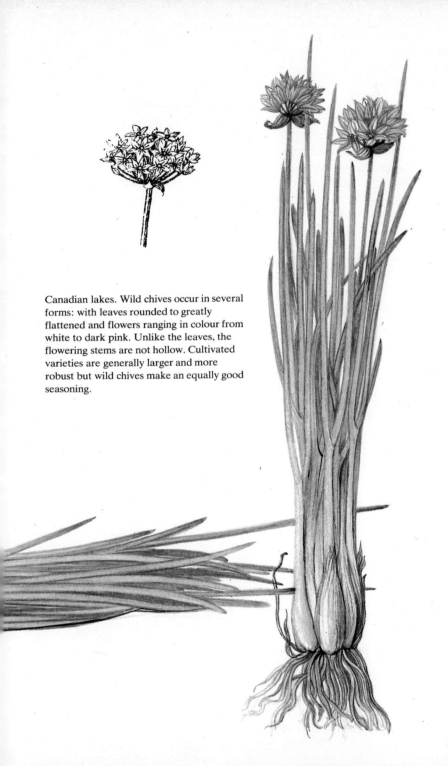

Canadian lakes. Wild chives occur in several
forms: with leaves rounded to greatly
flattened and flowers ranging in colour from
white to dark pink. Unlike the leaves, the
flowering stems are not hollow. Cultivated
varieties are generally larger and more
robust but wild chives make an equally good
seasoning.

Dill
Anethum graveolens

Dill is native to the Mediterranean region and its history goes way back to ancient times. It is mentioned in Egyptian inscriptions where it goes by the name of 'ammisi'. The Greeks and Romans, who spread it as far as the northern Alps during their campaigns, called it 'anethon' from which is derived the botanical name. In the year 812 Charlemagne, aware of its culinary and medicinal properties (the essential oil it contains is still used to relieve flatulence), ordered that it be grown on his estates. It was believed to silence rumblings in the stomach, stop hiccups, and prevent the formation of intestinal gas; burnt seeds if placed on a wound were said to promote rapid healing. Nowadays dill is naturalized and grown not only throughout Europe but also in America and the West Indies.

All the upper parts of the plant are aromatic, but it is the tender feathery leaves that have the most delicate aroma and pleasantly sour flavour. The fruits and the entire, unopened flower heads are also used as flavouring, especially for pickling gherkins, cabbage and onions. Dill is exceptionally good when combined with cream sauces and soups, cream cheese and butter, or with vinegar salad dressings. It is also used as a seasoning with raw vegetables, boiled meat and fish. A simple but tasty dish is boiled and buttered new potatoes or string beans with dill. As a rule it is not used with other herbs because of its distinctive aroma.

In order to have fresh dill in the garden the whole year round it should be sown in succession from March till late July. The leaves will be ready for picking within six weeks of sowing. Dill is an annual herb and plants sown in spring produce seeds in the autumn of the same year. Dill may be stored for the winter by chopping the leaves and preserving them in salt or vinegar.

It may also be dried, but this must be done rapidly and with care in an airy place at a temperature of not more than 30°C (86°F), otherwise the aromatic and extremely volatile essential oil will rapidly vaporize. This is also the reason why dill should be added to hot food just before serving. The dried herb should be stored in air-tight containers.

33

Roman or Common Chamomile   Compositae/Asteraceae
Anthemis nobilis

The scientific name of this perennial herb tells us that it bears 'noble flowers' (the Greek word 'anthemos' means flower and the Latin word 'nobilis' means noble). The flower heads, which have a spicy aroma and pleasant, slightly bitter taste, were originally used in the treatment of various diseases, including jaundice and diseases of the liver as well as migraine, as we can read in R. Banckes' medieval herbal. The French book on housekeeping *Le ménagier de Paris,* also from that period, recommends preparing a concoction from the flowers of chamomile and orange peel for rinsing the fingers at banquets. Chamomile tea is a time-honoured tonic with a pleasant taste that aids digestion. The main constituent of the flower heads is a pale-blue volatile oil similar to that found in German Chamomile *(Matricaria chamomilla).* Together with the bitter principles it gives the herb the distinctive flavour which is used in making liqueurs. In England the top parts of the plant are used to make herb beer and in the cosmetic industry it is used in the manufacture of shampoos.

Roman chamomile is native to the Mediterranean region but nowadays it grows wild in western Europe, including the British Isles, and is cultivated in Belgium, France and England. The simplest and most reliable method of propagation is by splitting up older clumps in spring, because the flowers are often sterile (do not produce seeds). The plants benefit by frequent transplanting.

1

Chamomile is commonly grown in the herb garden and because of its low growing habit can be used in place of grass. The double-flowered forms (1) in which most of the tubular florets have been replaced by tongue-shaped ray florets are generally cultivated nowadays. The commercially available herb usually consists of the flowers of the double form. The flowers are collected by hand in succession as soon as they are fully open and then dried as rapidly as possible in a well-ventilated place at a temperature not exceeding 30°C (86°F). They must be dried thoroughly to prevent spoiling caused by moisture condensation or overheating.

Chervil
Anthriscus cerefolium

Chervil is an annual herb growing up to 70 cm (2 ft 4 in). It is native to the Caucasus and western Asia and was used for seasoning food by the ancient Romans, who during their military campaigns introduced it to many European countries including the British Isles.

The leaves are a very delicate flavouring characteristic chiefly of the French cuisine. Because its aroma, reminiscent of a mixture of anise and parsley, evaporates readily, it should be added to hot dishes during the last stage of cooking, but best of all it should be used fresh.

Chervil combined with parsley, tarragon and chives make a *fines herbes* mixture used in omelettes. It is also used to flavour vegetables, meats (chiefly mutton), roast chicken and grilled fish. Chervil soup made of beef bouillon, cream and egg yolks was very popular at one time. On hot summer days chervil provides welcome variety when mixed with cream cheese or simply sprinkled on bread and butter. The leaves can be steeped in white wine vinegar to make a delicious salad dressing.

It is surprising how little chervil is grown on a commercial scale for it has no special requirements and its cultivation is relatively simple. However, it has widespread popularity with home gardeners in Europe as well as in north Africa, east Asia and America. Its glossy black seeds are sown outdoors in the ground where they are to grow. This should be a shaded spot for chervil does not tolerate sun-baked locations. To ensure a constant supply of foliage, cut out the flower stalks, for otherwise chervil dries up and dies after flowering.

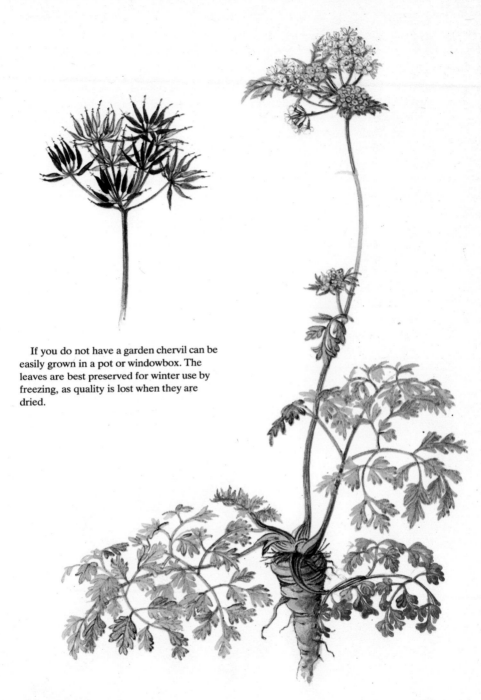

If you do not have a garden chervil can be easily grown in a pot or windowbox. The leaves are best preserved for winter use by freezing, as quality is lost when they are dried.

Celery

Apium graveolens

On the European continent celery is best known as a vegetable, used together with carrot and parsley root in soups, beef dishes, and in raw or cooked salads. It was already being grown for this purpose by gardeners of ancient times. The Greeks and Romans, however, cultivated some varieties with lush foliage and others grown for their delicate leaf stalks which were blanched by earthing up the plants as they grew. In those days celery was the symbol of grief and death. It was dedicated to the gods of the underworld, eaten at funeral banquets and woven into wreaths that were placed on graves.

The parts used primarily for seasoning are the strongly aromatic and slightly bitter seeds (achenes), which are grown and harvested for this purpose in France, India and the USA. The achenes, slightly reminiscent of the fruit of anise, are ground and combined with common salt for use as celery salt in seasoning foods. Some celery salts also include the ground root or foliage. Celery salt is used as seasoning for fish dishes, soups, vegetables and croquettes.

The leaves, too, may be used to flavour foods. They are cooked together with the stalks and removed before the food is served. If they are stripped from the thick stalks the leaves can be readily dried and used as seasoning in winter, for they retain their aroma if stored in air-tight containers. The foliage is also often used in the preparation of commercial soup mixes and various herb mixtures.

All the present varieties of celery were obtained by breeding and selecting from the original form with tough, slender, branching stems growing wild in salty soils, particularly on the south-European coast of the Mediterranean. Celery, like carrot and parsley, is a biennial herb but it is grown as an annual for use as a vegetable because in the second year it dies down after flowering when the seeds have ripened.

Angelica
Archangelica officinalis

Daucaceae

Angelica is a biennial though it sometimes continues growing for several years. It is the largest culinary herb, reaching a height of up to 2.5 m (8 ft). It grows wild in damp meadows and alongside water courses, mostly at higher altitudes. The first year it forms only a small rosette of leaves on the ground, the second year large leaves appear and tall, hollow, grooved stems bear large umbels of greenish-white flowers. The flowering period is during July and August. The fruits are ovate to elongate double achenes.

All parts of the plant are aromatic and have a strong, slightly bitter flavour. The ripe achenes are generally used as seasoning. These are collected by rubbing the dried umbels between the fingers. The rhizome is also used; this is about the size of a child's fist, from which grow numerous roots up to 30 cm (1 ft) long. It is dug up in autumn and dried slowly at a temperature not exceeding 35°C (95°F), the roots having been previously woven into a braid and wound around the rhizome. The roots, rhizome and fruits contain bitter principles, resin and other substances as well as an essential oil. They are used to flavour soups, gravies and salads.

The young green stems, cut into rounds and candied, are used to decorate cakes, and the roots to make liqueurs such as Chartreuse and Benedictine.

It is wise to wear gloves when handling the root, particularly in sunlight, for it may cause blisters on people with sensitive skin. In the Middle Ages the root was used as a remedy against poisoning.

Angelica is native to northern Eurasia and has also become naturalized in central Europe, where it was introduced in the 14th century from Scandinavia. In some countries (Belgium, Holland, Germany) it is cultivated in sunny locations with deep, moist, humus-rich soil. Propagation is by means of seeds (1) which must be exposed to frost and sun in order to germinate. That is why they are sown in autumn or early spring on the surface of the soil and left uncovered.

40

Horseradish

Brassicaceae

Armoracia rusticana

Horseradish has the most biting qualities of all the pungent culinary herbs belonging to the Brassica family, which include mustard, kohlrabi, garden cress and radish. In all probability it is native to southeastern Europe and western Asia and was introduced to central Europe by the Slavs during their mass westward migrations. Nowadays it is widely distributed throughout the world, often becoming established in the wild in sandy locations beside ponds and water courses. It was probably one of the 'bitter herbs' eaten by the Jews during the feast of Passover.

The fresh, finely-grated root is used as seasoning. A popular accompaniment for boiled meat is a thick cold sauce made of grated horseradish, salt and vinegar to which may be added grated apple, sugar and beef stock. Grated horseradish with cranberries and cream is very good served with game. Pure grated horseradish is excellent with hot sausages and boiled meats in place of mustard. Grated horseradish mixed with whipped cream and grated nuts is delicious with hot or cold ham. It is also used mixed with mustard. Cut in rounds the root is used for pickling gherkins and beetroots to make a tasty relish. Grated horseradish and prepared sauces may be kept in closed containers in the refrigerator for as long as 14 days without spoiling or losing their flavour because of the phytoncidic substances contained in the root.

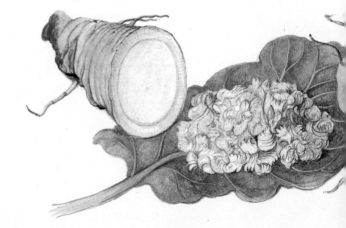

Horseradish is a perennial with a large, fleshy tap root. It is propagated only by vegetative means — by root cuttings. It is important to cut off the clusters of flowers so the plant's energies are concentrated into root development rather than fruit formation. The roots should be dug up in autumn or spring of the second or third year and stored in boxes in sand in a cool cellar so they do not dry out. Horseradish is very good for the health because of its high content of Vitamin C and mineral substances. One drawback with horseradish is that it can become an invasive weed; it should therefore be planted in a corner of the garden or beside the garden wall.

Southernwood, Old Man, Lad's Love   Compositae/Asteraceae
Artemisia abrotanum

Southernwood is a perennial sub-shrub that was very popular with the herbalists of medieval times. In Banckes' herbal we read that 'this herb burnt to ashes and mixed with oil will promote the growth of hair in persons affected by baldness' and the book *Hortus sanitatis* (meaning Garden of Health) further states that 'smoke from this plant has a pleasant scent and drives snakes out of the house'. It is used to this day as a home remedy to aid digestion and as an intestinal antiseptic.

The young aromatic foliage is used for culinary purposes, either fresh or dried. This has a bitter flavour, like the foliage of all members of the genus, and smells of lemon. It is used sparingly, mainly as seasoning for fatty pork and mutton, roast goose and duck, as well as to flavour pies, cream cheese, mayonnaise and salads. The French put parts of the plants in wardrobes believing they protect clothes against damage by moths and other insects.

Southernwood is native to the Mediterranean region and is probably only a cultivated form of the species *A. paniculata,* indigenous to southeastern Europe and the Middle East. Nowadays it has become widely established and also grows wild in Italy and Spain. It is often grown in gardens not only as a culinary and medicinal herb but also for its handsome foliage. Southernwood does not flower until late autumn in central Europe and generally does not produce viable seeds. It is therefore propagated by dividing older clumps. Old wood should be cut out during the dormant period in winter, thereby promoting the growth of new shoots and lush foliage in spring.

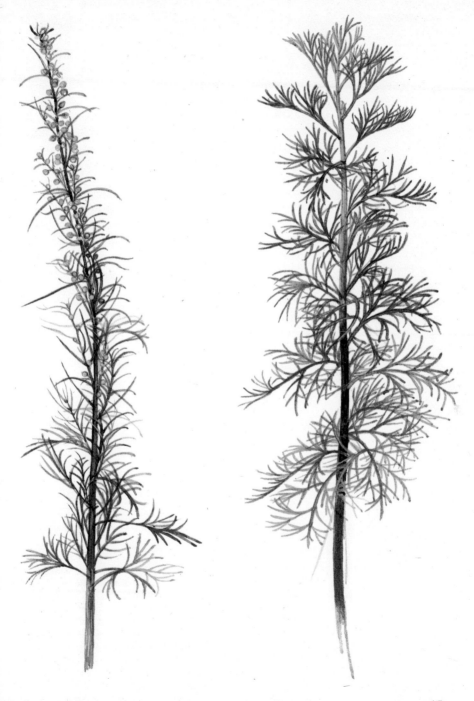

It is the tender foliage and non-woody top parts of the plant that are used, either fresh or dried, as seasoning. The specific name of this herb is derived from the Greek word *apinthion* meaning undrinkable, for it contains bitter principles which taken in excess are undigestible and may even have deleterious effects. What is harmful in excess, however, may often be beneficial in small doses. This is true of kitchen herbs in general and of wormwood in particular. For this reason only a few leaves are used as seasoning, mainly for boiled or roasted fatty meats, thereby not only improving their flavour but also making them more digestible. These properties have also made wormwood an important medicinal herb used by the pharmaceutical industry in preparations facilitating digestion. It was known in ancient times as we learn from the writings of Dioscorides and Pliny. In these we read that the winner of the quadriga races held at Roman feasts was given a drink of wormwood because the Romans believed good health to be an honourable reward. In medieval times it was also believed that the juice of wormwood mixed with sweet milk was effective 'against worms in the womb and in the ears'.

Wormwood is also used to flavour many bitter drinks including absinthe, vermouth and tonic water.

1

Wormwood is indigenous to the temperate regions of Europe and Asia. Often it becomes naturalized and may be found on untilled land, waysides, waste ground and rocky slopes. It is a woody perennial herb up to 130 cm (4 ft 6 in) high with leafy stems terminated by loose panicles of yellow flowers (1). The pinnate leaves are felted silvery-grey.

47

Tarragon Compositae/Asteraceae
Artemisia dracunculus

Tarragon is a perennial herb 60 to 120 cm (2 to 4 ft) high with entire, undivided, broadly linear leaves and tiny flowers.

The name *Artemisia* is apparently derived from Artemis, Greek goddess of the hunt and patron of virgins, for some *Artemisia* species have abortive properties. The specific name *dracunculus* is the Latin word meaning small dragon, or snake, probably in reference to the linear, tongue-shaped leaves.

The 13th-century Spanish physician and botanist Ibn Baithar states that fresh tarragon shoots were cooked with vegetables and the juice of tarragon was used to flavour beverages. He further writes that tarragon sweetens the breath, dulls the taste of bitter medicines and promotes sleep.

Nowadays it is used to make tarragon vinegar (a fresh sprig of tarragon put in a bottle of white or wine vinegar), tarragon mustard and pickled gherkins. It is widely used in Chinese and French dishes, especially with poultry, rice and poached fish, and in Béarnaise and Tartare sauces.

Tarragon grows beside rivers in southern and central Europe as well as western America. It thrives in humus-rich soils and warm, sheltered locations. Propagation is by division of older clumps or by means of offsets. The young shoots or leaves are used for seasoning. When harvesting, which may be carried out up to three times a year, cut 20- to 30-cm-(8-in to 1-ft-) long sections from the tops of the shoots before the flower buds open. It is at this stage that they contain the greatest amount of the essential oil that gives the herb its pleasant aroma and

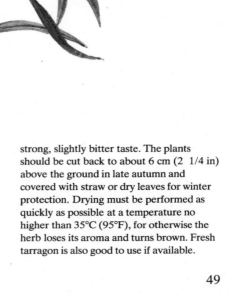

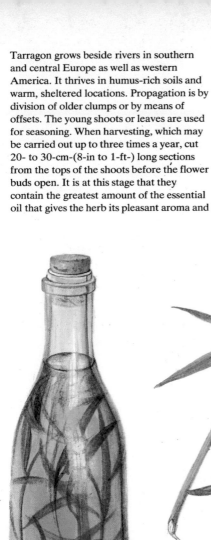

strong, slightly bitter taste. The plants should be cut back to about 6 cm (2 1/4 in) above the ground in late autumn and covered with straw or dry leaves for winter protection. Drying must be performed as quickly as possible at a temperature no higher than 35°C (95°F), for otherwise the herb loses its aroma and turns brown. Fresh tarragon is also good to use if available.

Mugwort
Artemisia vulgaris

Mugwort is a perennial herb reaching a height of up to 1.5 m (5 ft) and growing wild in a number of similar forms throughout the northern hemisphere — from the Mediterranean to Lapland, from India to Siberia, and from Mexico to Alaska. Hence the Latin name *vulgaris,* meaning common or widespread. It is grown mainly in the Balkan Peninsula, Italy, France and the USSR.

In former times mugwort was believed to have magical powers. In his herbal Mattioli wrote that superstitious people wore bands of this herb round their waists and wreaths on their heads on St John's Eve as a safeguard against the monsters, witchery, misfortunes and illnesses of the coming year.

Mugwort is used as seasoning for roast meat, especially pork and mutton, as well as roast goose and duck. It is sprinkled on the meat before cooking, but sparingly. In Spain it is used to flavour onion and vegetable soups as well as fish and fish soups. It is also good in salads.

Mugwort is easily grown from the seeds (achenes) even in poor soil. As a rule, however, this is unnecessary for it may be found growing wild on waste ground and by the wayside.

If it is to be used as seasoning then the tips of the young shoots must be harvested before the small flower-heads (1) open. The reason for this is that the amount of bitter principles rapidly increases during flowering, thus making the plant unsuitable for use as a culinary herb. The shoots are best dried tied into bunches and hung up in a well-ventilated place. The dried herb retains its pleasant aroma for a long time if stored in air-tight containers.

1

Sweet Woodruff

Asperula odorata

Rubiaceae

Sweet woodruff has whorled, rough-edged leaves, which give it its generic name *Asperula* − meaning rough. It has a pleasant fragrance, due to the presence of coumarin, when dried (hence the specific name *odorata*, meaning fragrant). It is a perennial herb with a creeping rhizome and tiny white flowers. Its range of distribution includes practically the whole of Europe, where it often forms dense undergrowth in deciduous woodlands. It is also found in western Asia and North America. If it does not grow wild nearby, it can be readily grown in the garden, either from seed or from young shoots detached and replanted during the flowering period. The top parts of the herb, either fresh or dried, have a number of uses. Drying must proceed slowly, at a temperature no greater than 35°C (95°F).

Nowadays woodruff is well-known as an essential ingredient of the German 'Maibowle'. This is prepared by steeping the young shoots in Rhine wine to which brandy and sugar or a piece of orange peel are sometimes added. The first record of this magical love and restorative potion, then called 'May wine', was made by a Benedictine monk in the year 854. In France it is the custom to add woodruff to champagne, whereas in Switzerland to cognac or Benedictine. In the United States it is used in making a May punch consisting of a mixture of wine, brandy and Benedictine. In northern Europe woodruff is used to flavour certain kinds of sausages and salamis.

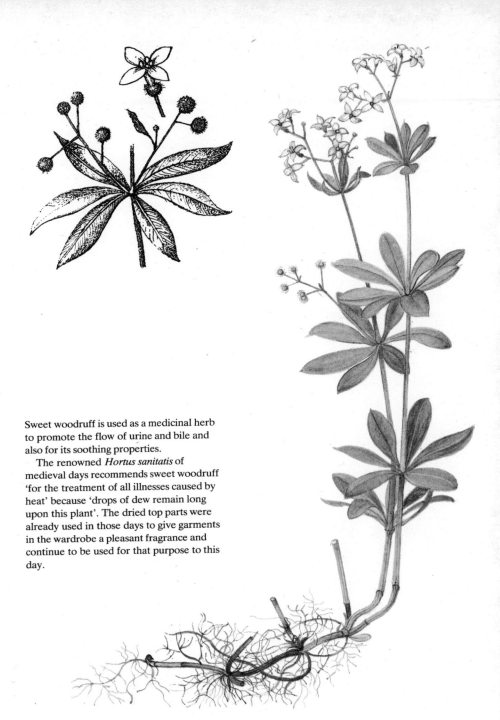

Sweet woodruff is used as a medicinal herb
to promote the flow of urine and bile and
also for its soothing properties.

The renowned *Hortus sanitatis* of
medieval days recommends sweet woodruff
'for the treatment of all illnesses caused by
heat' because 'drops of dew remain long
upon this plant'. The dried top parts were
already used in those days to give garments
in the wardrobe a pleasant fragrance and
continue to be used for that purpose to this
day.

Common Barberry
Berberis vulgaris

Berberidaceae

The common barberry is a spiny deciduous shrub up to 2 m (6 ft) high with upright branches and yellow flowers. When insects alight on the flowers they brush against the stamens. These curve inwards towards the pistil in the centre, thereby pollinating the plant. The fruits are bright red, fleshy berries that ripen in September and often remain on the shrub until late winter.

Nowadays it is a relatively rare shrub in the wild because it is a host plant of one stage of the life cycle of grain rust *(Puccinia graminis)* and thus not welcomed by farmers in the vicinity of grain fields, where it is systematically eradicated. This will doubtless soon lead to the disappearance of its sour, pleasantly astringent berries, which are used, the same as rowanberries, to flavour compotes and tarts, as well as piquant sauces for game and roast beef. They can also be made into a delicious juice or marmalade, or fermented to yield an excellent distillate. The dried sour berries in powdered form are good with grilled meats.

Barberry likes light and warmth, otherwise it has no special requirements and tolerates dry weather. That is why it is generally encountered in southern and central Europe, but it also grows wild in North America on rocky, sunny slopes, chiefly in lime-rich soils. It does not stand up well to harsh winters when it is damaged by frost. However, when the dead wood is cut back it will put out new shoots again from the base. The wood is lemon yellow and is used for inlaid decoration. The bark of barberry contains the poisonous alkaloid berberine, at one time used for dyeing in the leather industry.

Closely related to the common barberry are the decorative species of the same genus widely grown in gardens and parks. Some, for example *B. × stenophylla,* are not deciduous but retain their leaves throughout the winter.

Borage
Borago officinalis

Boraginaceae

Borage is an annual herb native to southwestern Europe. Because its blue flowers attract bees it is widely cultivated in bee-keeping regions, especially in England and France, but also in other parts of Europe, where it often becomes naturalized. It grows to a height of 60 cm (2 ft) and the young hairy leaves have a cucumber-like flavour. In the Middle Ages it was used together with mint, savory, parsley, garlic, fennel and rosemary to flavour salads and the flowers were used to garnish whipped cream, salads and soups. In those days it was believed to have a stimulating and exhilarating effect, hence the English saying 'borage brings courage'.

The fresh young leaves and entire top parts of the plant are harvested during the flowering period to be used as seasoning. Borage must always be finely chopped so the delicate hairs are not annoying. Borage is delicious by itself either cooked in butter or raw as a salad with lemon juice. As seasoning it is added to pickled gherkins and vegetables, to spinach and cabbage, mayonnaise, cold sauces and salads. It is also used to make herb butter, herb cream, cheeses and yogurt. It gives a refreshing cucumber flavour to iced fruit cups. It is also good with braised meat and fish dishes to which it is added just before serving. In Liguria (northern Italy) it is used as a filling for ravioli. The flowers are used to add aroma to vinegars.

Borage may be readily grown from seed, either in the garden or in a windowbox. Sow in spring after all danger of frost is past. Growth is rapid, its only requirement being a light soil with lime.

Dried borage is not suitable for culinary purposes but is used as a home remedy to prepare a decoction believed to cleanse the blood and strengthen the nerves and heart.

Black Mustard

Brassica nigra

Brassicaceae

The seeds of black mustard are prepared the same as those of white mustard *(Sinapsis alba)* to make a paste used as a condiment. Black mustard was known to most of the ancient peoples, who grew it as a vegetable and medicinal herb. Native to the eastern Mediterranean region, it was introduced to Europe by the Romans and is nowadays cultivated chiefly in England, Holland, Rumania, Italy and France, though not in such great quantities as white mustard.

The seeds of black mustard are brown to black and measure about 1.5 mm in diameter. They contain a large amount of oil used by the food industry. Prepared mustard is made by first pressing the oil from the seeds, then grinding the remains, or 'mustard cake', to a powder and blending it with liquid — grape juice in the case of prime-quality prepared mustards, otherwise vinegar or even plain water. The characteristic flavour of the various commercial kinds is determined by the other spices that are added to the mixture. The ancient Romans prepared mustard from seeds that had first been soaked in water and then crushed and boiled. According to another recipe the seeds were ground and then blended together with honey and oil.

The following is one of several recipes for those who would like to prepare their own mustard at home:

Ground black mustard seeds	500 g (17 1/2 oz)
Plain flour	100 g (3 1/2 oz)
Ground allspice	12 g (1/2 oz)
Ground cloves	2 g (a small pinch)
Ground ginger	5 g (a pinch)
Sugar	100 g (3 1/2 oz)
Salt	100 g (3 1/2 oz)

Blend with grape juice or vinegar to the required consistency. It is not necessary to follow this recipe exactly — you can adapt it to your own personal taste and experiment with whatever you fancy. It is used as a condiment with meat, sausages and salamis, and to flavour sauces.

Pot Marigold
Calendula officinalis

This is the well-known old-fashioned marigold of cottage gardens. It is a favourite garden flower because the flowering period is spread over summer and well into autumn, as indicated by the generic name derived from the Latin 'Kalendae', which in the ancient Roman calendar always marked the first day of the month. Its use as a herb actually came about by fraud, for in the days of the Roman Empire the poor used it in place of the costly saffron, a practice that continues to this day. It deserves to be forgiven, however, for its lovely colouring, called calendulin, is used as colouring matter not only in butter and cheese but also in soups, sauces and pastries. As everyone will agree food is enjoyed not only for its flavour and aroma but also for its visual appeal. Calendulin is soluble in fats, so if used to colour dough, marigold must first be boiled in milk.

The flowers were most popular in the Middle Ages when they were commonly used to colour food, mostly soups. They were believed to have healing properties: 'The mere sight of marigolds banishes a bad humour and strengthens the sight. Maidens make them into wreaths on their name-day and birthday to adorn their heads with their vivid reds and yellows.'

Pot marigold is native to southern Europe and the Orient and is noted for its ease of cultivation. It is an annual herb that is propagated in spring by sowing the seeds outdoors where the plants are to grow. The yellow-orange disc-shaped flowers are borne singly at the end of the stalk. The lingulate outer florets (1) are harvested for

1

use in the kitchen. These are arranged in
two or three rows and plucked when the
flowers are fully open. They must be dried
rapidly in shade to preserve the colour for
this fades when exposed to sunlight. The
dried flowers should be stored in a dark, dry,
well-ventilated place or in air-tight
containers. To this day the flowers are used
by the pharmaceutical industry in
antispasmodics and in preparations
promoting the healing of wounds.

Caper
Capparis spinosa

Caper is a prickly shrub with long, trailing branches growing on rocks and walls in the warmest regions of Europe and Africa bordering the Mediterranean since time immemorial. It was known to the ancient Greeks and Romans, but both Dioscorides and Galenos warned against the effects caused by eating the buds. In this they were wrong, however, for the buds are not poisonous and nowadays are used as an excellent flavouring for foods. The buds, produced in succession the whole summer long, are picked daily by hand and graded according to size. The spiciest, but likewise the most expensive, are the tiny, round, hard capers called 'nonpareilles', the cheapest are the so-called 'capucines', also known as 'capottes', which are up to six times larger. Medium-size capers are called 'surfines', 'fines' or 'mifines'.

Capers are a common seasoning of the Mediterranean peoples and widely used by them in their cooking. They may be used to flavour salads, mayonnaise and cold sauces and served with cheeses; their pungent aroma is not destroyed by cooking. The characteristic flavour of Mediterranean dishes may be achieved by combining capers with olives and onion. They are very good with braised or roast meats and above all with fish.

The fresh buds are unpleasantly bitter but drying destroys their pungent flavour. For this reason they are preserved by salting or better still by pickling in a vinegar solution. Most products are obtained from cultivated shrubs, grown chiefly in southern France, Spain, Italy and north Africa. Plantations are renewed after fifteen years, when the yield from aging shrubs begins to decline.

In the USSR capers are prepared from the related species. *C. herbacea,* which grows wild chiefly in the Crimea and Transcaucasia.

The flowers are followed by elongate, many-seeded berries (1).

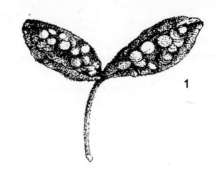

1

Sweet Pepper, Paprika

Capsicum annuum

Solanaceae

This sweet pepper, forerunner of the various cultivated forms of the present day, is probably native to Colombia and may still be found in South and Central America. It differs from the cultivated sorts by having small deciduous fruits. The dried and ground ripe berries are used for seasoning, especially those of the red forms with long, pointed fruits. The berries of the blunt-tipped forms and plump, tomato-like fleshy-walled peppers are harvested before they are ripe and eaten raw in salads or braised, roasted or preserved as a vegetable.

A characteristic constituent of capsicum is the strongly irritant alkaloid capsaicin, occurring most abundantly in the placenta partitions inside the berry to which the seeds are attached. The various cultivated forms differ in the amount of capsaicin they contain as do the seasonings of various provenance. The so-called 'Spanish paprika' is the sweetest variety, the seeds and partitions of which are carefully removed before grinding the fruit.

Paprika is one of the basic condiments of cookery. Without it there wouldn't be any Hungarian goulash. It is used in sauces, soups, salads, cheese spreads, sausages and salamis, as well as in meat and poultry dishes. It is one of the ingredients used to make tomato ketchup and curry-powder. Besides the dried ground seasoning, the tinned paste from the fresh ripe fruit is gaining widespread popularity.

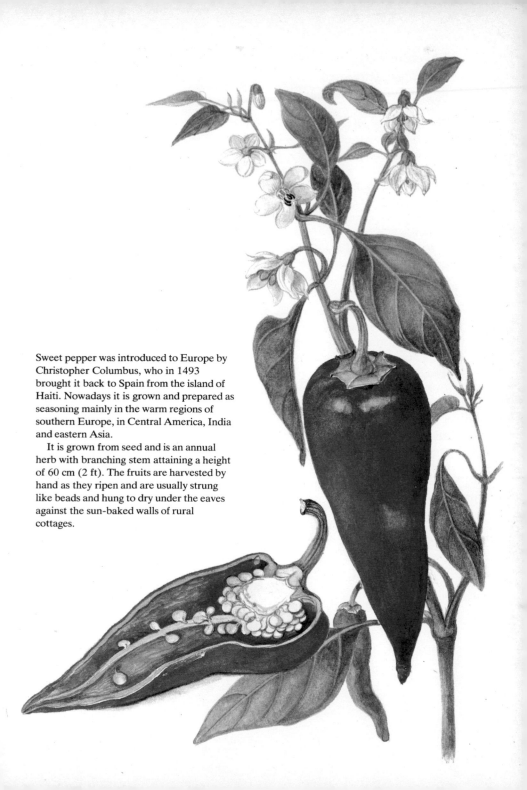

Sweet pepper was introduced to Europe by
Christopher Columbus, who in 1493
brought it back to Spain from the island of
Haiti. Nowadays it is grown and prepared as
seasoning mainly in the warm regions of
southern Europe, in Central America, India
and eastern Asia.

It is grown from seed and is an annual
herb with branching stem attaining a height
of 60 cm (2 ft). The fruits are harvested by
hand as they ripen and are usually strung
like beads and hung to dry under the eaves
against the sun-baked walls of rural
cottages.

Cayenne Pepper, Chilli
Capsicum frutescens

Solanaceae

The hottest of all seasonings is that obtained from the ripe fruits (berries) of various forms of *Capsicum frutescens*. Called chillies, they are bright red, much smaller than the fruits of sweet pepper and vary in shape, depending on the variety. The fruits are generally dried in the sun, becoming wrinkled during the process and turning dark red to orange red. The dried fruits, with calyces removed, are ground to yield cayenne pepper, so named after the port of Cayenne, chief town of French Guiana.

The plant is native to tropical America and must have been grown there long before the discovery of the New World, as it has been found in ancient Peruvian graves. The Spaniards and Portuguese who discovered this seasoning on their voyages and introduced it to Europe called it 'Indian pepper'. Nowadays it is cultivated in most tropical countries, primarily in India and Thailand. Though it is a perennial herb reaching a height of more than 1 m (3 ft) in the tropics, in Europe it is grown in the greenhouse as an annual. In the tropics, field crops are renewed every third or fourth year.

Whole fruits are used in pickled vegetables; when ground, they are an essential ingredient of curry-powder. Hot tabasco sauce, used in the same way as Worcestershire sauce, is prepared by boiling the chopped fruits in salt water or vinegar. Chillies are a spice typical of South American cookery with a great many uses (with meats, fish, shellfish, soups, sauces, eggs and vegetable dishes).

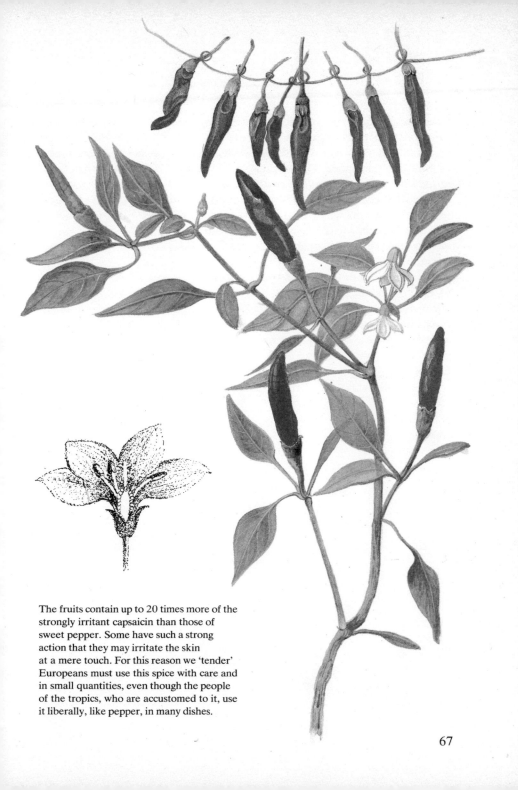

The fruits contain up to 20 times more of the strongly irritant capsaicin than those of sweet pepper. Some have such a strong action that they may irritate the skin at a mere touch. For this reason we 'tender' Europeans must use this spice with care and in small quantities, even though the people of the tropics, who are accustomed to it, use it liberally, like pepper, in many dishes.

67

Caraway
Carum carvi

Daucaceae

The fruits of caraway were found during archeological excavations in the ruins of circular dwellings dating from the third millenium B.C. and are probably the oldest spice used in Europe. In Asia, too, caraway was grown in pre-Christian times. Dioscorides recommended it for the stomach and in the Middle Ages it was the custom to end a feast with 'caraway cookies', apparently because caraway has very good carminative properties (relieving flatulence), for which purpose it is used in pharmaceutics to this day. It was used together with anise, coriander and fennel to flavour jams, and as we learn from Shakespeare's Falstaff it could also be used to flavour baked apples.

Nowadays caraway is commonly used in breads and on buns, also added to boiled potatoes, sauerkraut, roast pork and roast goose or duck. In Germany it is used as a flavouring for Kümmel, the popular liqueur. According to medieval tradition, chopped fresh leaves are added to soups and salads. Caraway may also be used in powdered form, but it must be ground just before being used so the fragrant essential oil does not evaporate.

Caraway is a biennial plant indigenous to a wide area embracing almost all of Europe and Asia. Because of its large consumption it is nowadays grown as a field crop throughout most of Europe as well as in Asia and north Africa. It does not tolerate wet, heavy clay soils. The seeds are sown in spring about 2 cm (3/4 in) deep in drills 40 cm (16 in) apart. It is harvested the second year in late summer when two-thirds of the fruits have ripened. The cut plants are tied into sheaves and left in the field until they are dry and fully ripened, after which they are threshed to obtain the seeds. The seeds — achenes (1) — are usually dried by natural heat. Caraway growing wild in the meadow is just as good for flavouring as the cultivated form.

Costmary

Chrysanthemum balsamita

Compositae/Asteraceae

Costmary, native to the Middle East, was known to the ancient Egyptians, Greeks and Romans, who probably introduced it via Europe to England. Nowadays it grows wild in the eastern and mid-western United States, where it was introduced by the colonists.

The one-time fame of this herb is documented by its many different common names. In the USA it was called 'bibleleaf' because the first colonists used the long leaves as bookmarks for the bible. In England it was used to flavour ale, hence the name alecost. The German name Marienkraut, meaning costmary, is now only a reminder of an almost forgotten spice, once highly prized and widely grown in gardens. The parts used for flavouring are the large leathery leaves with an aroma slightly reminiscent of menthol. They are used fresh or dried to flavour soups, salads, pies, stuffings for fatty meats, poultry, game and especially veal.

Costmary is a hardy perennial herb that survives winter weather well. The leaves grow mainly on the lower part of the shoots and lusher foliage may be obtained by removing the large, much-branched flower stalk before the flowers open. It is readily propagated by dividing large clumps, any time from spring until autumn. The lower, long-stalked leaves are harvested.

After cutting off the stalks the leaf blades should be dried at a moderate temperature in a well-ventilated place. The dry leaves are then crumbled or ground and stored in air-tight containers. Because the foliage is highly aromatic it should be used sparingly.

Sachets filled with a mixture of dried costmary and lavender are placed between linen to give it a pleasant scent. Also popular is tea made from costmary.

Chicory, Succory
Cichorium intybus

Compositae/Asteraceae

From as far back as the 16th century the roots of this perennial herb have been ground to make a pleasant-tasting, slightly bitter substitute for coffee used in coffee-mixes and liquid 'coffee' extracts. Extract from the root is also used to flavour certain refreshing soft drinks. Varieties with thick roots such as *C.i. radicosum* are bred and cultivated for this purpose. These are cut in autumn, dried, ground, and then lightly roasted. Roasting causes chemical changes that give chicory a pleasant flavour and aroma. Chicory is sweet because the root contains inulin, which during the roasting process turns to fructose and caramel, which gives the dark brown colour.

Besides varieties with thick roots there is also a variety *C.i. foliosum* which is grown as a vegetable for use in salads. It is forced during the winter in sand in a dark cellar, or in a frame covered to exclude all light, for chicon production. The chicons are tender, pale yellow and have a mildly bitter taste. Salads are also prepared from other cultivated varieties that have not the slightest resemblance to the type species; one such being 'cicoria di Treviso' with decorative red foliage, which is very popular in Italy and Switzerland.

Roasted, ground chicory root and chicory salad also have medicinal properties. Both promote the flow of bile and aid digestion. The roots of wild chicory are used for the same purpose in pharmaceutical preparations. Wild chicory is nowadays distributed throughout Europe, north Africa and in Asia as far as Lake Baikal; however, it is not known where it originated.

Cinnamon
Cinnamomum zeylanicum

Lauraceae

Cinnamon is obtained from a number of trees and shrubs belonging to this genus and native to southeast Asia. The most delicately scented spice, however, is a very costly article obtained from the Ceylon cinnamon. Because of its high price, due to the extremely complicated method of preparation, it was slow in establishing itself as an article of commerce. It was not till the second half of the 18th century that the first plantation was founded in Ceylon, home of the parent plant, by one of the Dutch settlers. Whereas in the forests Ceylon cinnamon is a tree attaining a height of 10 m (33 ft), on plantations it is cut down close to the ground so it continually puts out new shoots which grow to a length of 2 m (6 ft) in two years. The bark is peeled from the severed shoots (to a length of about 1 m (3 ft), the outer layer (cork and primary bark) carefully scraped off, and the remaining bark then dried. As it dries the thin layer of cleaned bark curls into a cylinder. The separate 'quills' are slipped inside each other in bunches of ten and then cut to the same length.

To this day Sri Lanka is the principal producer of Ceylon cinnamon, even though its cultivation has spread to southern India, the Seychelles, Madagascar, Martinique, Jamaica, French Guiana and Brazil.

Much cheaper than Ceylon cinnamon (1) is Chinese cinnamon (2) from southern China. As we learn from the herbal of the Chinese Emperor Shen-nung, dating from about 2,800 B.C., cinnamon was used as a spice in China 5,000 years ago. Chinese cinnamon is obtained by peeling the bark from seven-year-old branches of the Chinese cinnamon tree *(Cinnamomum cassia)*, scraping off the greater part of the corky layer and then drying the remainder. It is sold in pieces 1 to 3 mm (about 1/10 in) thick, 2 to 5 cm (3/4 to 2 in) wide, and up to 40 cm (16 in) long, which have a grainy fracture and are usually only slightly rolled inward.

2

Cinnamon is used whole, broken into small pieces, or more commonly ground, as flavouring for sweet dishes, puddings, gingerbread and compotes. It is also an ingredient of ketchup and curry-powder, and is used together with cloves and lemon peel in making mulled wine.

1

Lemon
Citrus limonia

Lemon is a small, evergreen tree that produces flowers and fruits throughout the year, so that a single specimen has blossoms, green fruits and ripe yellow fruits at the same time. The structure of the lemon is best seen in a cross-section. Inside is a juicy pulp divided into as many as 15 sections, usually without seeds. The pericarp is composed of two layers, a white, spongy inner layer (albedo) and an outer cover or rind (flavedo), coloured yellow when ripe and containing numerous large cells filled with the essential oil of lemon which gives the peel its characteristic smell. It is obtained by carefully peeling the rind of fully-ripened lemons; this may be dried and then crumbled and stored in air-tight containers for later use. More commonly used is the grated peel of fresh lemons. It is recommended to use only the peel of lemons that have not been sprayed with chemical preparations (lemons are sometimes sprayed with fungicides to prevent rotting and decay during long-term transport and storage; these substances are usually poisonous not only to fungi but to man as well and cannot be removed even by thorough washing).

Lemon peel gives foods a refreshing aroma and is used in pastries, candies and compotes. The essential oil of lemon is obtained for industrial purposes by pressing (prime quality) or distillation (lower quality). Besides the peel, lemons also provide juice that is a rich source of Vitamin C and can be used in place of vinegar. Its acidity is due to the presence of citric acid so that it can be used even by those who cannot tolerate vinegar. Also its scent is far less penetrating than that of vinegar.

In all probability the lemon is native to Iran.
Since the time when it began to be cultivated
in Persia in the 6th century B.C. and three
centuries later in Greece and Italy, growers
have developed countless cultivated forms
and nowadays we no longer even know what
a wild lemon looked like. Its cultivation
spread from Greece and Italy to all the lands
of the Mediterranean region and later also
to practically all the subtropical regions of
the world.

Lemon is closely related to orange *(Citrus
aurantium)*, whose subspecies *C. a. amara*
bears small, round, bitter fruits which are
used in making orange marmalade, very
popular especially in England.

Coffee
Coffea arabica

Coffee is most probably native to Ethiopia where the tree was first cultivated and its seeds used as a beverage sometime in the 13th century. From there the custom of drinking coffee spread to Arabia and Iran. From Egypt it was introduced to England, but not until the turn of the 16th and 17th century. Nowadays it is mainly produced in South America, with Brazil heading the list. Other coffee-raising countries are Java, Yemen, India and Sri Lanka.

The greatest quantity is used in the preparation of various sorts of black coffee, which is nothing more than water flavoured with coffee. About one-third of the world population has become addicted to this beverage which is not surprising, for not only does it have a pleasant flavour and aroma but also a mildly stimulating effect, apart from its importance as a social and cultural custom. Otherwise coffee is used to flavour milk, puddings, custards, cakes and ice cream, generally in the form of filtered coffee made with boiling water. The best flavour and aroma, however, is obtained by steeping coarsely ground coffee in fresh cream at room temperature. Though it takes longer this method preserves the finest aromatic substances which would otherwise evaporate.

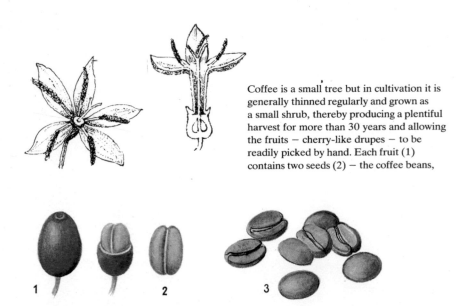

Coffee is a small tree but in cultivation it is generally thinned regularly and grown as a small shrub, thereby producing a plentiful harvest for more than 30 years and allowing the fruits — cherry-like drupes — to be readily picked by hand. Each fruit (1) contains two seeds (2) — the coffee beans,

1   2   3

encased in a parchment-like coat. After they
are harvested the ripe fruits are dried in the
sun and then mechanically hulled. The dry
seeds (3) have a bland flavour, acquiring
their aroma and colour by roasting, when
the sugar they contain is caramelized and
the beans turn brown. Roasting must be
brief and rapid, only a few minutes at
a temperature of 200°C (616°F), after which
the coffee beans must be cooled fast to
prevent the aromatic substances produced
by the roasting process from evaporating.
For the same reason coffee should be
ground just before use.

Cola acuminata Sterculiaceae

Chewing cola nuts is a widespread habit amongst the inhabitants of the whole of north Africa. It is a form of more or less harmless drug addiction that might be compared to drinking black coffee or tea.

The term 'cola nuts', however, is not correct from the botanical point of view for the fruits of the cola trees are not nuts with a hard woody shell but spherical capsules resembling an orange and composed of five follicles (1), each of which contains several seeds (2), the size of a pigeon's egg. Fresh seeds from ripe fruits are more effective than dry seeds and for that reason the natives put them in baskets with damp moss. They contain approximately 2% caffeine, which is gradually released as they are chewed; at first they have a bitter flavour which gradually becomes sweet. Also released during chewing is a red pigment that colours the lips. Dried and ground cola nuts may be used to make a hot beverage in the same way as coffee. In Europe the extract from the nuts *(Semen Colae)* is used in pharmaceutical preparations and in soft drinks, also to flavour and colour certain wines, and as flavouring for creams, chocolate and liqueurs.

Cola is a tree resembling the horse chestnut. It is native to tropical central and west Africa, where it forms groves, and is raised in the West Indies, Brazil and tropical Asia. It is closely related to coffee, whose seeds likewise contain caffeine, and its flowers grow directly from the trunk or older branches (cauliflory) as in coffee.

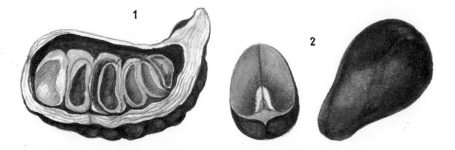

Coriander
Coriandrum sativum

Daucaceae

Coriander is a cultivated annual or biennial herb native, most probably, to the eastern Mediterranean. Long ago, it spread to southern Asia and Europe, where it often grows wild as an escape. Finds in old Egyptian graves confirm that it was used by the Egyptians. The Greeks and Romans likewise used it not only to flavour foods and wines but also as a medicinal plant. It was probably the Romans who introduced it to the British Isles. In the Middle Ages it was a popular flavouring for wines and marmalades as well as soups and meat dishes. Mattioli recommends it for flavouring smoked meat.

The name of the plant, which was used by Pliny, is derived from the Greek words 'koris', meaning bed-bug, and 'annon', meaning anise, for when rubbed between the fingers the fresh leaves smell of bed-bugs. Nevertheless, the fruits, cleverly combined with other spices, give some foods a pleasant and unusual taste. It is used in making breads and in herb mixtures for flavouring salamis and pâtés. Coriander is most widely used in the Spanish-speaking countries of South America. It is one of the ingredients of curry-powder and is also added to pickled vegetables and to flavour certain herb liqueurs, such as gin. Fresh young leaves are also used as a seasoning.

The plant is closely related to caraway, fennel, dill and anise. The coriander sold in shops is from cultivated plants. It is raised mainly on the coast of north Africa, chiefly in Morocco, as well as in Europe, India, North and South America, principally in Argentina. The ripe fruits (1) have a sweetish, slightly pungent flavour and a pleasant aroma.

1

Cornelian Cherry

Cornus mas

Cornaceae

Cornelian cherry is one of the first shrubs to bloom in central Europe, its small yellow flowers, arranged in capitula, appearing as early as March. Because few can resist breaking off a sprig of this herald of spring, it is in danger of becoming an extinct species in the wild. It is dying out even though it will grow almost anywhere, tolerating dry conditions as well as limy soil and the air pollution of cities. It is, however, being planted in parks and gardens.

Cornelian cherry is one of the few shrubs whose fruits, like those of juniper and barberry, are used to flavour foods. They are red, barrel-shaped drupes that are sour at first. Even though the shrub flowers in early spring the fruits ripen in late autumn, remaining on the shrub well into winter and turning sweet only after the first frost. Inside the pulp is a hard seed which, when sown, does not germinate until the second year. They are used both fresh and dried to flavour apple and pear compotes, which are otherwise bland, and also in sauces served with game and grilled meats. In the Balkans they are distilled to make an alcoholic liqueur.

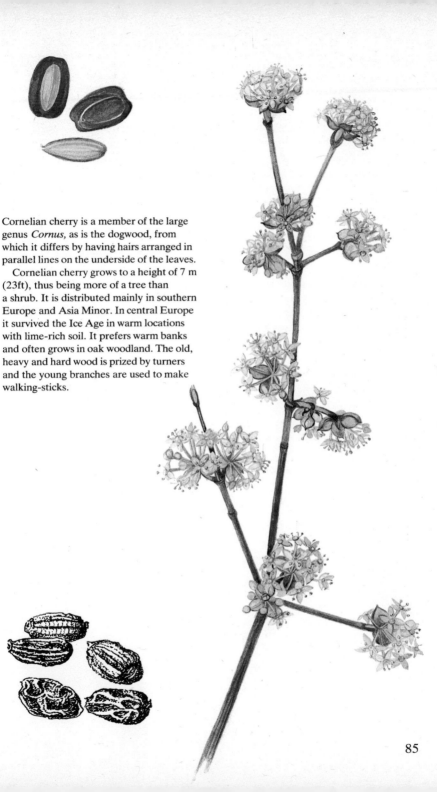

Cornelian cherry is a member of the large genus *Cornus,* as is the dogwood, from which it differs by having hairs arranged in parallel lines on the underside of the leaves.

Cornelian cherry grows to a height of 7 m (23ft), thus being more of a tree than a shrub. It is distributed mainly in southern Europe and Asia Minor. In central Europe it survived the Ice Age in warm locations with lime-rich soil. It prefers warm banks and often grows in oak woodland. The old, heavy and hard wood is prized by turners and the young branches are used to make walking-sticks.

Saffron

Crocus sativum

Fragrant dye or culinary herb that colours? It is hard to say, for saffron is a perfect synthesis of the two. There is no disputing the fact that originally saffron was used as a dye. Babylonian and Persian rulers wore saffron-coloured shoes and the ladies of ancient times used it to colour their robes. But by the Middle Ages already one-third of all central European recipes for dishes served in wealthy families called for saffron. Henry VIII of England was so fond of saffron in his kitchen that he forbade its use as a hair-dye by the ladies of the court.

Used for flavouring are the bright orange, trifid stigmas that must be snipped out by hand, together with a part of the style, as soon as the flowers open and then dried quickly and very carefully. What a laborious and tedious task this is, is best documented by the fact that it is necessary to collect and process stigmas from as many as 200,000 flowers to obtain 1 kg (2 lb 4 oz) of dried herbs. That is also why it is so expensive and hence the saying 'as costly as saffron'. In medieval times its adulteration by other admixtures was punished by burning the culprit at the stake or burying him alive.

Only a small pinch of saffron needs to be added to foods to give them a golden colour as well as an indescribable aroma. The colouring matter is so strong that two stigmas suffice to colour as much as three litres of water. Except in Spain, European cookery nowadays uses saffron in only a few dishes, but in those it is essential. These are mainly bouillabaisse, poached fish, paella, risotto Milanese and saffron cakes.

In Europe saffron was first raised in Spain, where it was introduced by the Arabs when they established their Andalusian domains in southern Spain from the 9th century onward. Its cultivation then spread to other European countries but only in Spain and southern France did it continue to be raised on a larger scale. Spanish saffron is also considered to be the best on the market.

Saffron greatly resembles the
spring-flowering species of crocus — *Crocus
heuffelianus* and *C. vernus* — the one great
difference being that it flowers in autumn, as
does the highly poisonous autumn crocus
(Colchicum autumnale). Beware of
mistaking the one for the other!

Cumin
Cuminum cyminum

Cumin resembles caraway, with which it is closely related, in aroma and flavour, but it is much more pungent and quite bitter. In olden times it was more highly prized than caraway, as testified to by the fact that, according to the Bible, the Pharisees paid their tithes with it and even in medieval England vassals used it to pay the feudal lords in lieu of their services. It was also well known to the ancient Greeks, Romans and Egyptians, who used it in place of pepper. Its fruits were put in graves together with other gifts for the dead. Theophrastus tells us that cumin was grown for culinary use and advises that sowing of the seeds be accompanied by cursing to ward off evil spirits, which would otherwise damage the germinating plants. On old Egyptian papyrus rolls it goes by the name of 'tapnen'.

In the Middle Ages cumin was a culinary herb of the aristocracy, popular mainly for seasoning poultry. It was believed to destroy gases and other foul things in the stomach. One medieval dish called 'Comminée de Poulaille' consisted of chicken cooked in water and wine, then roasted and finely chopped together with ginger, sour fruit juice, saffron and cumin. Nowadays cumin is one of the ingredients of curry-powder. By itself it is also a popular seasoning in Indonesian cookery and is likewise commonly used in Latin America and north Africa.

Unlike caraway, cumin is an annual herb with white or reddish flowers, borne in umbels. The fruits are used for seasoning; these are double achenes up to 6 mm (1/4 in) long, which often remain joined. Cumin grows wild in Turkestan and is raised commercially chiefly on the coast of north Africa, in Malta, Sicily, the Middle East and India. Even though it is also available already ground, it is best to stock it whole and grind it just before use so it does not lose its aroma.

89

Turmeric
Curcuma longa

Zingiberaceae

Turmeric is a tropical plant, native to southeast India, which was introduced to Europe by Arabian merchants in ancient times. The aromatic rhizome is used as a condiment. It contains a vivid orange-yellow pigment which earned the plant the name 'Indian saffron'. Unlike saffron the pigment in turmeric is soluble in fats. It is quite harmless and is used to colour butter, margarine, cheeses and mustard. By reason of its colour as well as its strong, pronounced flavour, turmeric is one of the principal ingredients of curry-powder, Worcestershire sauce and numerous other seasonings.

Turmeric is not a common seasoning in Europe, apart from England; whereas in the United States it is widely used in scrambled eggs, cream sauces, mayonnaises, various spreads and fish salads. It is particularly good on grilled chicken, not only masking the odour of the poultry farm, which is unpleasant to many people, but also giving it a lovely golden colour. It is also used with all fried meats. Indian cookery uses turmeric to colour rice and sweet dishes. Once you become accustomed to this condiment you will be partial to it for ever.

Turmeric is a perennial plant resembling reeds and growing to a height of 1 m (3 ft). It is cultivated in China, India, the West Indies and Java. It is propagated by means of thin pieces of the rhizome called 'fingers' and can be harvested within ten months of planting.

Harvested rhizomes are washed, then boiling water is poured over them and after that they are dried by the heat of the sun. During this process the pigment spreads to the surrounding tissues, giving the entire rhizome the colour by which it is judged on the market and the rhizome hardens so that it can be ground to a fine powder. Rhizomes are divided into shorter thicker sections ('curcuma rotunda') and up to 8-cm- (3-in-) long, finger-like side shoots ('curcuma longa').

90

Cardamom
Elettaria cardamomum

Zingiberaceae

Cardamom is one of the finest spices and also one of the most expensive. From Dioscorides and Pliny we know that it was used by the ancient Greeks and Romans. In the Middle Ages people believed it had medicinal properties that would heal practically every disease. It is the seeds of this perennial plant that are used as a spice. It is native to southern India and Sri Lanka and also raised nowadays in Central America, particularly in Guatemala. Cardamom is used mostly by the peoples who grow it as is also the case with many other herbs and spices. It is used by the Arabs to flavour so-called Bedouin coffee, which in Saudi Arabia is a symbol of hospitality. It is also popular, however, in Scandinavia, where it is used to flavour sausages and salamis and meat dishes. In addition to that it may be used in pickling vegetables and marinating fish, as well as in pastries and liqueurs.

The plant's leafy stems are up to 3 m (10 ft) high, the clusters of flowers (racemes) grow from the axils of bracts on stems that are much shorter. Propagation is by seeds, or, as in ginger, by root cuttings. The fruits are triloculate capsules (1) that ripen in succession throughout most of the year. They are harvested before they are ripe and dried carefully in the sun or by artificial heat so they do not burst and the seeds (2) retain their delicate aroma. This is how the spice is sold on the market, the seeds being removed from the capsules just before use. These seeds have a sweetish, but spicy flavour. They are often supplied to shops in powdered form, which is quite unsuitable for the aroma is rapidly lost.

Commercial cardamom is of two kinds: one from Malabar with small fruits and seeds, the other from Mysore with fruits and seeds that are slightly larger.

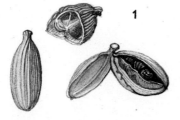

1

2

Rocket
Eruca sativa

Brassicaceae

Rocket, like many other herbs, is native to southern Europe and western Asia, but nowadays it is naturalized in central Europe through Spain to Morocco and through Asia Minor to Turkestan. It is one of the oldest cultivated plants and has given rise to numerous forms still grown around the Mediterranean. The leaves and seeds were already used by the Romans as seasoning and it was also popular in England during the reign of Elizabeth I.

Nowadays rocket is mostly eaten as a salad, chiefly in southern France, Italy and Egypt; it is also used to season green salads and beans to which it gives a pleasant, slightly bitter flavour. The tender, juicy young leaves may be minced and used the same as chives in sandwiches, in cream cheeses, on boiled, buttered potatoes and as a garnish on cold meats. The ovate seeds, up to 1.5 mm (1/20 in) long, are used in Iran, India, Greece, southern France and Spain to make a very pungent mustard.

The seeds of rocket are rich in oil (30%) and this is the main reason for which it is raised nowadays. The oil is obtained by pressing; it has a golden yellow colour and after being stored for several months loses its sharp, biting quality.

It is exceptionally good for pickling vegetables. Rocket is an annual herb reaching a height of 50 cm (20 in). The terminal inflorescence is composed of white or yellowish flowers with dark violet or pink veins.

94

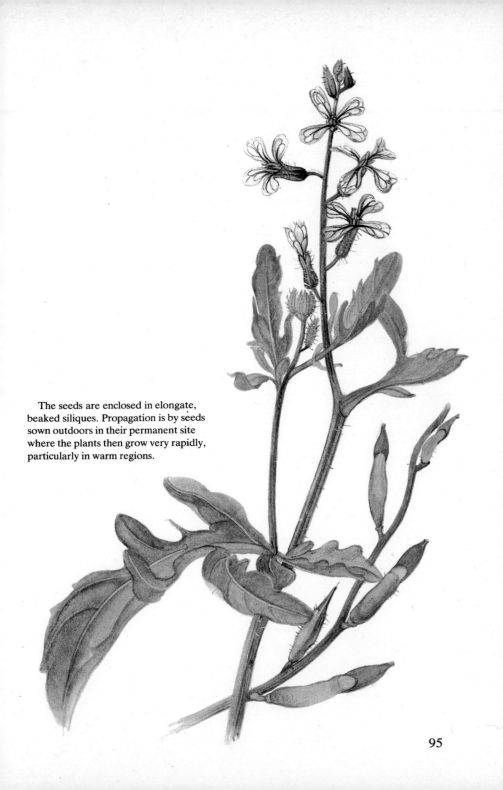

The seeds are enclosed in elongate, beaked siliques. Propagation is by seeds sown outdoors in their permanent site where the plants then grow very rapidly, particularly in warm regions.

95

Clove
Eugenia caryophyllata

Clove is the dried flower bud of a tropical evergreen tree, native of the Moluccas, which reaches a height of 20 m (65 ft). It was known in the Far East and in India in ancient times and was shipped from there by the Chinese as far back as 400 B.C. For centuries it was used to alleviate toothache and also to sweeten the breath. However, it was not until the 5th century A.D. that it began to be shipped to Europe from Alexandria, being sold there by Arabian merchants. From the 9th century onwards clove became a fashionable spice used by wealthy families.

The first European to see the tree growing in its native land was the Venetian merchant Marco Polo in the 13th century. When Vasco da Gama discovered the Molucca Islands the Arabian monopoly was replaced by the Portuguese and in the 17th century by the Dutch. Up until the turn of the 18th century the entire world was supplied with cloves only from the Moluccas. In 1770 the French, under threat of death, smuggled some seeds on two small ships and grew the first cultivated trees on the islands of Mauritius and Réunion. Nowadays cloves are produced chiefly in Zanzibar and Pemba, where they have been raised since the early 19th century.

The terminal inflorescences with unopened buds are harvested by hand, using ladders, and then dried in the sun, which turns them a dark colour.

Cloves contain a large quantity of an essential oil that is very aromatic but loses its aroma with long storage. A good way of testing the quality is to put the spice in water; if it is of good quality it will sink or else float upright, stale cloves float flat on the surface. They are used either whole or ground to flavour sweet dishes and pastries, also in meat dishes, marinated fish, liqueurs and mulled wine. The oil has a medicinal value in that it stimulates the appetite and aids digestion; because of its high content of eugenol, it also has an antiseptic effect.

97

Fennel

Daucaceae

Foeniculum vulgare

Fennel was a popular herb among the Chinese, Indians, Egyptians, Greeks and Romans in ancient times, when it was believed to have miraculous healing powers 'against all fevers'. It reached Europe in the early Middle Ages, where it was introduced by the Romans.

Fennel is native to the Mediterranean but it has become naturalized in many countries of the temperate zone. It is raised commercially in France, Germany, Italy, Poland and Romania, as well as in the USSR, China and Japan and Argentina. It is also grown on a small scale in herb gardens. The leaves are used to flavour fish soups and sauces and in salads. In Italy it is preserved in vinegar and salt and eaten as a vegetable (Italian dill). The seeds are used to flavour bread (similar to anise), sprinkled on rolls, in pickling gherkins and vegetables and in vegetable dishes. Italians sprinkle ground fennel on barbecued meat. The seeds yield an oil used in pastry making and liqueurs promoting digestion, and are used by the pharmaceutical industry in the preparation of gargles.

In the Middle Ages fennel had all sorts of uses. The fruits were used to flavour sweets, fish sauces and soups. It was recommended for the treatment of cataracts, worms in the ears, and to promote the flow of milk from the breast. The following recipe is for 'cold brewit': 'take mush made from almonds, dry it on a cloth and when dry put it in a vessel; to this add salt, sugar, the white powder of ginger and juice from fennel along with wine'.

Fennel is generally grown as a biennial. The seeds — double achenes — are sown outdoors in the open in July. If properly tended plants may yield seeds for three to four successive years.

1   **2**   **3**

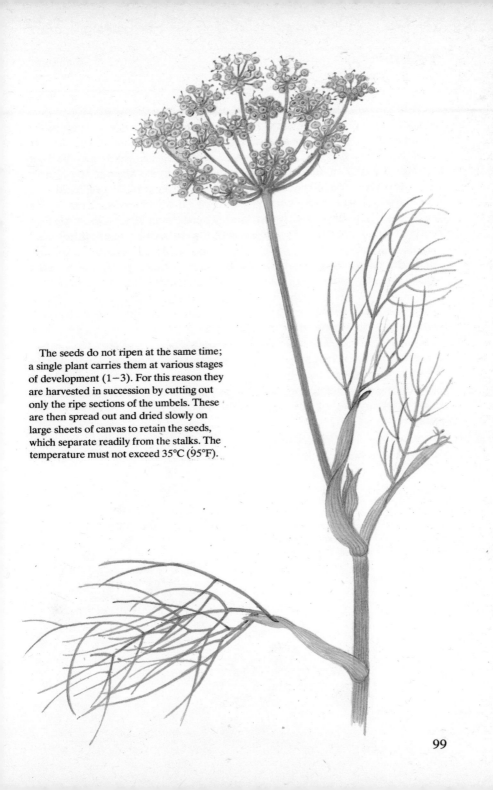

The seeds do not ripen at the same time; a single plant carries them at various stages of development (1—3). For this reason they are harvested in succession by cutting out only the ripe sections of the umbels. These are then spread out and dried slowly on large sheets of canvas to retain the seeds, which separate readily from the stalks. The temperature must not exceed 35°C (95°F).

Soy Bean
Glycine soja

Soy bean is one of the oldest cultivated plants in the world. It is native to southeast Asia and China where it has been raised from as far back as 3,000 B.C., which makes it all the more remarkable that Europe, where it was introduced as a curiosity in the late 18th century, showed no interest in it until the 19th. From then on, however, its spread was rapid and nowadays it is the most widely grown of all leguminous plants, being raised over huge areas of arable land. The seeds contain a great deal of protein (40%), similar in composition to that of meat, and are thus a very nutritious food.

For the purposes of this book the beans are of interest as raw material for making soy sauce. Its preparation is relatively lengthy and complex. Cooked soy beans are mixed with salt and wheat or barley flour and fermented much the same as wine; the resulting product is then strained, yielding a dark-brown liquid that improves with age.

Soy sauce is an age-old flavouring of Chinese cookery. In the 5th century B.C. the recipe was brought by a Buddhist monk to Japan, where it also rapidly gained widespread popularity. In our modern day and age it is becoming increasingly popular not only in Europe but also in America. It is likewise one of the ingredients used in making Worcestershire sauce.

Cultivated forms differ in the colour of their seeds (1). In regions where soy bean is grown on a large scale the proteins are extracted from the beans and made up into various kinds of synthetic meat products.

1

They are also used to make a very
nourishing flour, particularly good for
baking and for making nougat-type sweets.
Last, but not least, some ten million tons
a year are processed for use as vegetable oil
for cooking, the remaining products being
used as a very nutritious protein food for
livestock.

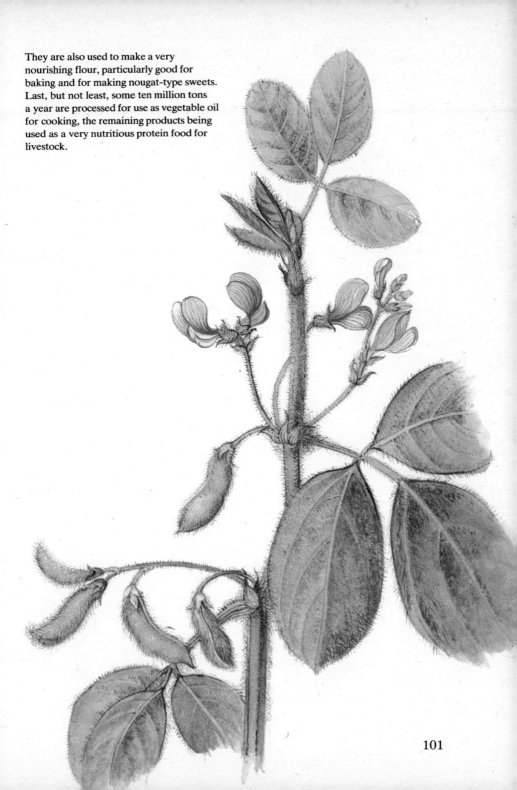

Licorice
Glycyrrhiza glabra

Christ himself chewed 'sweet wood' as a child – the peeled root of licorice ('glykas' in Greek means sweet and 'rhiza' means root). Licorice grows wild in southern Europe, the Middle East, Asia Minor and Afghanistan, and is raised commercially in the USSR, France, Belgium, Spain, Germany and elsewhere.

The dried and ground roots are used for flavouring, or better still the extract from these roots, sometimes thickened to syrup-like consistency so it will not spoil and can be stored. Licorice was made famous by the town of Pontefract in East Yorkshire, where it was raised and processed commercially before the town became an industrial centre. Pontefract cakes and other sweets from licorice are made there to this day, but from imported, not home-grown roots. The liquid extract may also be used in making delicate sweet drinks and to disguise the unpleasant taste of some drugs. In Victorian times it was the custom to eat licorice every Friday as a purgative.

Black lozenges called 'succus liquiritiae', made from the residue obtained after evaporating off the water in which licorice root has been boiled, not only have a pleasant spicy flavour but also dissolve mucus and thus act as an expectorant. For this reason licorice is also used in medicine.

Licorice is a perennial herb up to 180 cm (5 ft 6 in) high with a long, spindle-shaped root (1), which is why it does best in deep soil that is not too heavy. Propagation is usually by means of root suckers, shoots or parts of the underground stems because the seeds are very slow to germinate and generally have poor germination.

The roots are dug up in the autumn of the third year, washed, peeled and dried slowly. They are sweet and have a characteristic but faint smell.

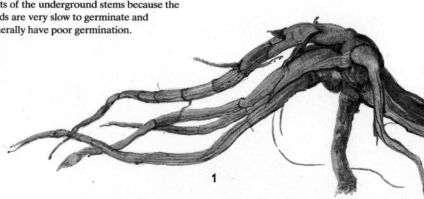

1

103

Common Hop

Humulus lupulus

Hop is native to Europe and western Asia. It was used originally as a medicinal herb by the ancient Greeks and Romans. The first to use it in brewing beer were probably the people living in Mesopotamia between the Euphrates and Tigris rivers in olden days. We learn about the first hop-fields in Europe from a deed of donation issued by the Frankish king Pépin III 'the Short' in the year 768 A.D. when hops began to be cultivated by monks in the monasteries, where beer was brewed. From that time on the cultivation of hops spread not only in Europe but also in North America, Australia and New Zealand as the consumption of beer grew throughout the world.

The female flowers are used almost exclusively in the brewing of beer, to which they not only impart a pleasant bitter taste but, because of the resin present in the lupulin, also prevent the multiplication of bacteria that cause lactic fermentation which spoils the beer. Tender young hop shoots were at one time eaten as a salad or boiled like asparagus.

1

Hops are a dioecious plant with stems which twine in a clockwise direction. Only the female plants are cultivated, however, and if any male plants are found in the vicinity of hop fields they must be destroyed to prevent pollination and the development of fruits which would spoil the crop. Hops are raised in fields where they climb up a system of wires and poles to a height of 10 m (33 ft). They are perennial but only the roots overwinter, putting up new shoots again in spring. Hops are propagated by means of cuttings from these shoots. The female flowers or strobiles (1), covered with glossy greenish-yellow glands containing bitter and resinous lupulin, ripen in late summer. They are harvested mechanically and dried by artificial heat on mesh sheets in drying sheds.

Hyssop
Hyssopus officinalis

The name hyssop was given to a number of different plants in olden times. The name itself tells us why this happened. It is derived from the Greek words 'hys', meaning pig, and 'ops', meaning face. Many plants of the Lamiaceae (Labiatae) family have flowers that resemble a pig's snout.

Hyssop is native to the Mediterranean region and central Asia and was introduced to central Europe in the 10th century by the Benedictine monks. In medieval times it was a popular kitchen herb, its leaves being used in soups, pickled vegetables, meat pâtés and poultry stuffings. It is used to this day in European cookery for its sweet smell reminiscent of camphor for flavouring vegetable soups, salads, sauces and meat dishes, including game. Hyssop is also a medicinal plant used to aid digestion and to limit sweating, for which reason it is apparently used in the Orient in preparing the slightly alcoholic beverage called sherbet. It is also used in flavouring many liqueurs such as Chartreuse. Hyssop is attractive to bees and is grown in gardens for its mass of fragrant blue flowers.

Hyssop is a perennial, branching sub-shrub
that turns woody at the base and reaches
a height of 50 cm (20 in). Still grown widely
for its many uses, it has no special growing
requirements but prefers a sunny situation
and lime-rich soil.

The flowers appear in late summer and
early autumn, which is also when the plant is
harvested by cutting the flowering parts that
are not yet woody. Because it contains
essential oils hyssop should be dried at
a temperature not exceeding 35°C (95°F).

Star Anise
Illicium verum

The spice is obtained from an evergreen tree which grows to about 8 m (26 ft) high and is native to southeastern China. It is a very ancient tree belonging to a primitive family. In China, where it was known long before the Christian era, it was one of the most popular of spices along with cinnamon. However it was not until the late 16th century that is was first brought to Europe by the English navigator Sir Thomas Cavendish.

The relatively large flowers, growing from the leaf axils, are followed by a compound fruit (a follicle), fleshy at first, later becoming woody and forming an attractive star with anise-like fragrance (hence the common name star anise). The ripe follicles burst on the ventral side to release the single seed contained in each. They are harvested when ripe and then dried. The seeds have a pungent, spicy flavour.

Star anise is sold in shops both whole and ground, but it is used for flavouring only in powdered form, like anise, chiefly in sweet dishes and coffee-cakes, in plum and pear compotes, and to flavour candies. It is also an ingredient of ground spice mixtures for flavouring puréed fruits and tarts. It is a typical spice of Chinese cookery, used chiefly with young pork and duck, and is an ingredient of soy sauce. It is also used to flavour aromatic liqueurs such as anisette.

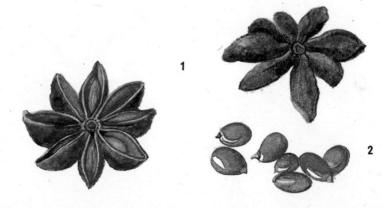

1

2

Star anise is grown not only for its fruits (1) and the spice they yield but also for the lovely reddish wood prized by cabinet makers, joiners and turners.

The seeds (2) are sown in nurseries and the young plants grown in plantations or in avenues alongside highways.

Common Juniper
Juniperus communis

The common juniper is a branching, evergreen, coniferous shrub from 9 to 12 m (30 to 40 ft) tall. The needles are arranged in whorls of three and are usually 1 to 2 cm (1/2 to 1 in) long and 1 to 2 mm (about 1/10 in) wide. The juniper is a dioecious species, i.e. individual shrubs bear only male, or only female flowers. The former are elongate catkins (1), the latter inconspicuous round cones (2) which mature into berry-like cones called juniper berries (3); these are green the first year, turning blue-black with a greyish bloom the second year. Inside are three hard seeds. Good quality seasoning must not contain unripe berries or ones that are coloured brown.

Besides essential oil (as much as 2%) the berries contain a bitter-tasting mixture of tannins, resins and other organic acids, which gives them their characteristic woodland aroma and spicy bitter flavour. It is perhaps for this reason that juniper was a popular flavouring with huntsmen as an essential in preparing game. It may, however, also be used for marinating fish, with fatty meats, and to disguise the odour of cabbage or beets. It is the principal flavouring and aromatic substance in gin. Ground juniper berries are often an ingredient of special herb mixtures.

Common juniper is distributed throughout
practically the whole of the northern
hemisphere from lowlands high up into the
mountains. Propagation is by means of
seeds, which germinate only after being
exposed to frost. The fruits are harvested by
hand. Gloves should be worn when doing
this to prevent the prickly needles damaging
the hands. The harvested berries are dried in
thin layers in a shaded, well-ventilated spot
at a temperature not exceeding 35°C
(95°F) for otherwise they lose their
potency.

Orange Milk-cup
Lactarius deliciosus

Russulaceae

Orange milk-cup is one of the most piquant of all mushrooms. Up until the middle of this century it was no problem to make for the young spruce woods in autumn, crawl under the bottom branches and gather the glossy orange caps growing all around. Nowadays, due apparently to intensive forestry practices, extensive use of pesticides and fungicides, and last but not least environmental pollution, the orange milk-cup is hard to find and in all probability the day is not far off when it will become extinct. Unless we learn to cultivate it before then, we shall be deprived forever of its inimitable flavour and aroma, which is even more powerful when pickled in vinegar. It is not suitable for drying. Fresh or pickled mushrooms give a delicious spicy flavour to vegetable dishes, potato soup, goulash and other stewed meats as well as to omelettes. Pickled mushrooms are served as a side-dish together with roast meats and risottos. Orange milk-cup can also be used to make an excellent ketchup.

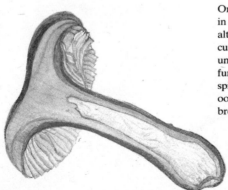

Orange milk-cup generally grows in groups in young, moist spruce woods at higher altitudes. The caps of young mushrooms curve under, spreading as they develop until, in the adult form, they are funnel-shaped. They can be identified by the spicy aroma and bright orange milk that oozes from the wound when a piece is broken off.

112

113

Bay, Wreath Laurel
Laurus nobilis

Bay, or laurel, is a symbol of fame and victory. A wreath of bay leaves was a token of honour given to poets and conquerors of antiquity and has remained so to this day. Apollo, the sun god of the Greeks and Romans, regarded as the perfection of masculine beauty, was depicted with a laurel wreath on his head. Caesar wore such a wreath on his triumphal marches, and modern-day winners of grand prix races are likewise honoured.

The poet's or wreath laurel is an evergreen tree native to the Mediterranean where it occurs as a relic of the Tertiary flora. It has simple, leathery leaves in the axils of which grow bunches of whitish flowers from which develop blue-black berries.

The first course at medieval feasts was often boiled apples and large Provençale figs baked with bay leaves. Bay leaves together with orange peel were also used to scent water for rinsing the fingers at the table. Nowadays they are used chiefly in savory dishes, cream sauces, marinades for meat, pickling vegetables and mushrooms and poaching fish. They may also be used sparingly in soups, stews and pig's-foot jelly.

Nowadays laurel is grown not only in the Mediterranean countries but also in many other parts of Europe. Two-year-old leaves (1), up to 10 cm (4 in) long and 3 cm (1 in) wide, are harvested in the autumn and dried in thin layers in shade to preserve their characteristic aroma and flavour. This pleasant, slightly bitter flavour is due to the presence of an essential oil containing pinene, eugenol and cinene. Good quality bay leaves should be without stalks and the blades should be pale green, not greyish or dark brown.

Small laurel trees are often grown in wooden tubs, trimmed into shapes and used to decorate the patio or porch. Propagation is by means of seeds, which germinate rapidly if sown immediately after the ripe fruits (2) are harvested; or by means of stem cuttings. Laurel may be grown indoors in a mixture of 1 part sand, 1 part garden soil and 1 part peat, thus providing their owner with a constant supply of fresh bay leaves.

115

Lavender
Lavandula officinalis

Lamiaceae

Lavender is native to the warm limestone slopes of the Mediterranean coastal regions. It is one of the most highly perfumed of all plants and the essential oil, obtained from the unopened flower spikes, is used by the cosmetic industry in making perfumes, soaps and shampoos. These uses are apparent in its botanical name, for the Latin word 'lavare' means to wash, and lavender was used by the Romans to perfume their bathwater. Nowadays it is raised for this purpose chiefly in Hungary, Yugoslavia and France.

The flowers are highly perfumed and therefore only the foliage, which is less aromatic, is used in cookery. It is bitter and very spicy and one has to become accustomed to it. This is probably the reason why it is not widely used in European cookery. The leaves may be used with roast mutton, braised meat, fish and fish soups, as well as in salads and with vegetables. They are also an ingredient of southern herb mixtures.

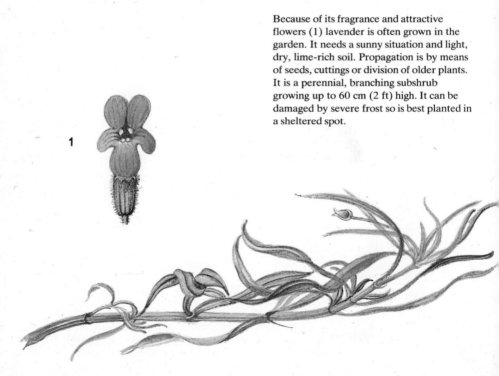

Because of its fragrance and attractive flowers (1) lavender is often grown in the garden. It needs a sunny situation and light, dry, lime-rich soil. Propagation is by means of seeds, cuttings or division of older plants. It is a perennial, branching subshrub growing up to 60 cm (2 ft) high. It can be damaged by severe frost so is best planted in a sheltered spot.

1

It should be lightly clipped when flowering is over so that it will send up a profusion of new shoots again the following spring. Leaves stripped from the twigs should be dried at a moderate temperature.

In the Middle Ages lavender was regarded as a treasure. The wealthy used it to give their clothes a pleasant scent and to repel moths. *Hortus sanitatis* recommends placing a sachet containing a mixture of lavender flowers, laurel leaves, rose petals, marjoram, cloves, nutmeg and stachys on the head for the alleviation of all types of pain.

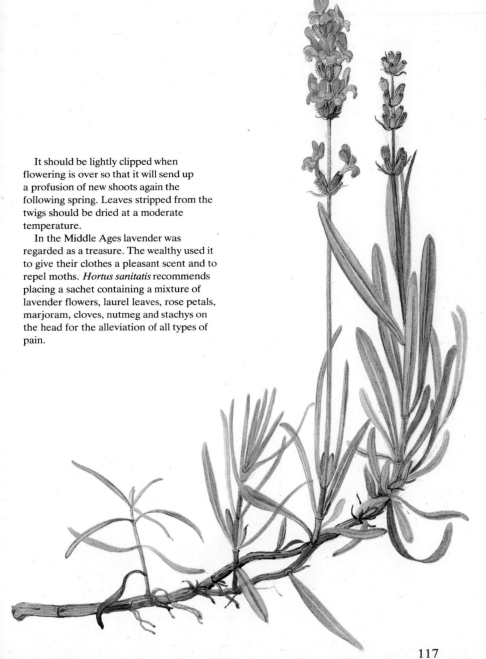

Garden Cress

Lepidium sativum

Brassicaceae

Garden cress, native to north Africa and western Asia, is an annual herb about 60 cm (2 ft) high. It was one of the kitchen herbs known to the Romans and it was they who introduced it to the rest of Europe. Until recently, however, it remained a forgotten herb of the past, and only occasionally is it found growing wild in waste places. It did not attract renewed interest until after the Second World War but now it is common to grow the young plants in the home throughout the year. It is especially welcome when there are not many fresh greens to be had to make an aromatic salad that stimulates the appetite and is rich in Vitamin C. Cress may also be used to flavour other salads and also as a garnish for cold dishes and with cheese. It is generally not mixed with other seasonings and is used fresh, because cooking results in the loss of vitamins as well of the pleasant, mildly pungent flavour, which is replaced by an unpleasant odour.

Young plants may be obtained quickly by sowing the seeds in dishes in soil, or simply on a piece of wet cotton or flannel on a plate. They should be sown on the surface, which should be kept moist all the time. When the seeds have swollen they form a thick layer of mucilage and then rapidly sprout, so that within two weeks you can harvest young plants with two true leaves. Up to this point they need no feeding, for they have an ample store inside the seeds. Seeds may be sown in succession at 14-day intervals throughout the year.

Lovage
Levisticum officinalis

The original form of lovage is the closely related species *L. persicum* which grows wild in the hills of southern Iran. It was known to the ancient Greeks and Romans, hence the generic name, derived from the Latin word 'ligusticum' because it grew in abundance in Liguria, a region in northwestern Italy. It was also popular in the Middle Ages, as we learn from the records of Hildegarde, abbess at the Rupertsberg abbey in the 12th century, mainly as a medicine for treating a wide variety of diseases. After that it slowly fell into oblivion, surviving only in country gardens, whence it is currently making a rapid comeback.

The fresh or dried leaves, roots and fruits are used for flavouring. The aroma and flavour are similar to that of commercial meat extract and the leaves are therefore added to soups, mainly beef soup. However, they are equally good added to sauces, vegetables, salads and roast meats. The fruits (double achenes) are used in pickling mixed vegetables and gherkins, as well as in bread and on cheese sticks. The rhizomes and roots are used to make commercial soup flavourings. The hollow stem may be cut crosswise into ring-like pieces and candied in the same way as the stem of angelica. All parts of lovage may be used fresh as well as dried, whole, crushed or ground.

Lovage is a large perennial herb up to 2 m (6 ft) high with a fleshy rhizome and long, branching roots. It grows best in moist deep soil. It may be propagated by seeds, but for the herb garden a single offset detached from the parent plant will suffice. Parts should be dried at a temperature no greater than 35°C (95°F) for the plant contains essential oils, and stored in air-tight containers.

Tomato
Lycopersicum esculentum

Solanaceae

The tomato was included in this book on culinary herbs with some misgivings, but as the basic ingredient of various kinds of ketchup it deserves to be mentioned. It is a native of northwestern South America (Peru and Ecuador), where the Incas raised it probably in ancient times, as did the Aztecs in Mexico. In the 16th century the tomato was taken from Mexico to Spain, where its Aztec name 'tumantl' was changed to tomato, the name by which it is known in many other languages.

The first European botanist to describe the plant was Mattioli. He named it 'mala insana', meaning unhealthy fruit, and for a long time it was considered poisonous. In consequence it was not eaten until the 19th century. Mattioli was partly right, for the green parts of the plant are slightly poisonous and furthermore he was perhaps guided by a well-founded fear; for the tomato belongs to the nightshade family which includes many highly poisonous species which it resembles.

Tomato is a perennial herb but is grown as an annual. It is a creeping plant and so is trained up low supports to keep the fruits clean. The method of raising tomatoes has been worked out to the minutest detail and enables very high yields to be obtained (depending on the climate).

Though the tomato's use in Europe is fairly recent, this universal fruit, used as a vegetable, salad, flavouring and food colouring, rapidly became one of the most widespread commercial crops in the world. Intensive breeding led to the development of numerous cultivated forms of different shapes, colours and flavours. Unfortunately the most important commercial varieties, those that bear large, round and regular, smooth-skinned fruits which can be successfully transported, have the poorest flavour. When using them in salads the flavour must be enhanced with vinegar and other dressings. Therefore, do not always judge tomatoes by the way they look; those with the superior flavour are not always the best looking.

Sweet Marjoram
Majorana hortensis

Lamiaceae

Even the smallest herb garden should include at least a few marjoram plants. The one difficulty is that, being a native of the warm Mediterranean region, it is damaged by frost in colder winters and must be sown afresh every spring. However, it is well worth it, for the dried herb from the shop cannot begin to compare with freshly chopped leaves sprinkled on soup or on a potato pancake.

As a plant of the Mediterranean region marjoram was known to the ancient Egyptians, Greeks and Romans, who used it not only to flavour food but also prized it as a miraculous herb with the power of healing practically all diseases, especially colds and chills.

In the Middle Ages it was grown for its fragrance and beauty. Before hops were known, it was used in brewing beer and in France to make a wine called 'hippocras'. It was also added to water used to rinse the fingers at the table during banquets. Nowadays, marjoram is added to soups, sauces for stewed meats (mainly mutton), stuffings and pâtés. Its widest use, however, is in seasoning sausages and salamis. Sometimes it is used together with other fresh herbs in 'bouquet garni'.

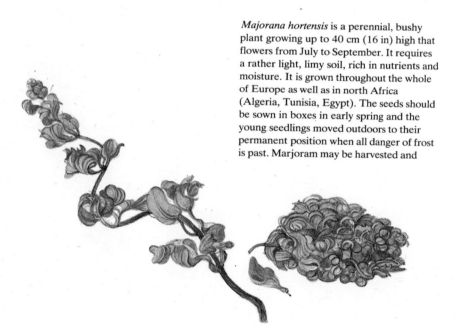

Majorana hortensis is a perennial, bushy plant growing up to 40 cm (16 in) high that flowers from July to September. It requires a rather light, limy soil, rich in nutrients and moisture. It is grown throughout the whole of Europe as well as in north Africa (Algeria, Tunisia, Egypt). The seeds should be sown in boxes in early spring and the young seedlings moved outdoors to their permanent position when all danger of frost is past. Marjoram may be harvested and dried in early summer before flowering. Cut the foliage off about 6 cm (2 1/4 in) above the ground; it will put out new shoots and yield another crop in autumn. This time pull up the whole plants, tie them in bunches and dry them slowly in a shaded, well-ventilated spot to preserve the aroma. Strip the leaves and flower remnants from the dry stems. Discard the stems, for they would spoil the quality of the seasoning, and store the rest in air-tight containers.

Fairy ring Champignon
Marasmius oreades

Tricholomataceae

These inconspicuous mushrooms are still commonly found in meadows and other grassy places in the temperate regions of Europe, despite the wide use of artificial fertilizers and chemicals to increase crop yields. They are most numerous following a rainfall after the hay harvest. They generally grow in clumps and often form fairy rings which can measure as much as several metres in diameter.

Whole mushrooms are easily dried; when reconstituted they rapidly regain their original form and taste like fresh mushrooms. Dried mushrooms may be stored in air-tight containers for several years. The whole caps previously immersed in water are used for seasoning. Properly dried mushrooms can easily be ground to a powder, which can be stored. Fairy ring champignon is used like other mushrooms to flavour soups, sauces and meat dishes as well as in pickled vegetable relishes.

Fairy ring champignon *(M. oreades* – 1) is closely related to *M. scorodonius* (2,3), from which it differs by certain morphological features and chiefly in flavour and aroma. The former is slightly larger with thicker stem up to 8 cm (3 in) high and cap up to 6 cm (2 1/4 in) across.

Unlike *M. scorodonius,* which has a brown cap and dark brown stem, fairy ring champignon is a dingy white colour all over. Its flavour resembles a mixture of mushrooms and nuts. *M. scorodonius* can be easily identified by the penetrating garlic odour and it is used in the same way as garlic for flavouring.

3

Lemon Balm, Bee Balm
Melissa officinalis

Balm is native to the eastern Mediterranean. It was raised by the Romans two thousand years ago; they spread the plant to other parts of Europe including Great Britain. Nowadays it is grown throughout southern Europe and the Middle East, Germany and elsewhere. It readily becomes naturalized as an escape.

Balm is a perennial herb up to 60 cm (2 ft) high. The leaves have a delicate lemon flavour. They are added alone or with other herbs to omelettes, salads, fish and rice. In Belgium and Holland they are used to give a more delicate flavour to pickled herring and eels. Balm is also a popular ingredient of herbal teas, aromatic wine cups and refreshing ice-cold drinks. Spaniards add balm to soups and sauces and to flavour milk. The leaves added to a cup of hot tea give it a lemon flavour without the sour taste. The delicate lemon aroma, however, evaporates rapidly and thus the herb should be added at the last minute to cooked food. Dried leaves lose their aroma after a time, even if stored in an air-tight container.

1

It is recommended to grow balm in the herb garden and use the fragrant leaves (1) fresh. Seedlings grown from seeds should be planted out in deep open fertile soil in a sunny spot. Leaves for winter use should be picked before the flowering period begins when they contain the greatest amount of the fragrant essential oil. They should be dried carefully in a shaded and well-ventilated spot. Balm is also useful to bee-keepers for it is much visited by bees, as indicated by its Greek name *melissa,* meaning bearing honey, and its common name Bee Balm. Besides propagation by seeds, balm may also be multiplied by division of older clumps.

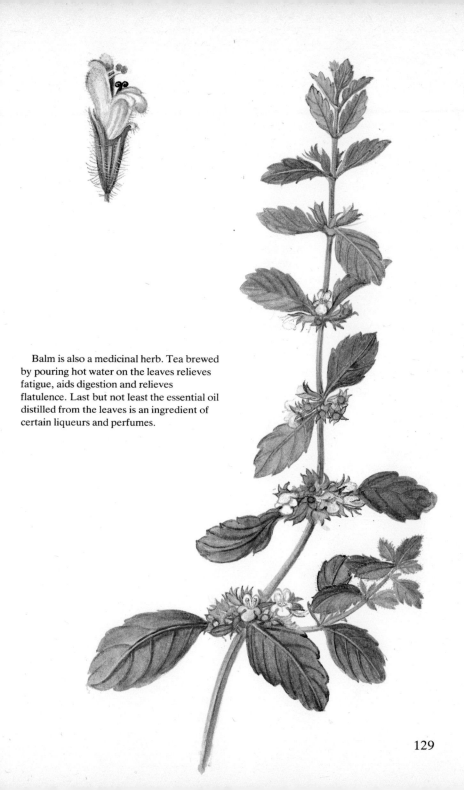

Balm is also a medicinal herb. Tea brewed by pouring hot water on the leaves relieves fatigue, aids digestion and relieves flatulence. Last but not least the essential oil distilled from the leaves is an ingredient of certain liqueurs and perfumes.

129

Peppermint
Mentha piperita

Lamiaceae

An anonymous writer of the 9th century A.D. writes that there are as many kinds of mint as there are sparks flying from the mouth of a volcano, and in the Middle Ages there were probably just as many uses. We come across it in many recipes for widely diverse meat dishes, omelettes, salads and sauces. There are indeed a great many species, peppermint being the best known.

Both the fresh and dried leaves are used as a flavouring. As a rule, mint is not combined with other herbs. It enhances fruit salads, beverages and puddings; especially in the hot summer months, for it leaves a pleasant cool sensation in the mouth and freshens the breath. Nowadays it is used only rarely with meats, usually with mutton, but is excellent with various vegetables such as cucumbers, tomatoes and potatoes as well as legumes. Mint tea, which does not need to be sweetened, is very tasty and healthy. It promotes the secretion of gastric juices and bile thus aiding digestion and lessening flatulence. Mint thus combines properties that are not only satisfying to the palate but of medicinal value as well. Britain's classic mint sauce, served with lamb, however, is not made from peppermint but from spearmint *(M. spicata)*, whose essential oil is also used in making chewing gum.

Peppermint is a multiple hybrid obtained by complex breeding and selection from the two species, *M. aquatica* and *M. spicata.* For this reason it may be propagated only by vegetative means, by division, for the seeds would produce widely varied offspring, mostly of poor quality and often with a repugnant odour. The principal component of the essential oil contained in the leaves is menthol, well-known ingredient of mouthwashes, toothpastes and candies.

Peppermint is a perennial herb, up to 1 m (3 ft) high, grown throughout Europe in a number of forms. These range from those with all-green leaves to forms with red stems and undersides of the leaves. Leaves are collected at the beginning of the flowering period and dried immediately as rapidly as possible in a warm airy place.

Nutmeg, Mace
Myristica fragrans

Nutmeg is an evergreen tree growing up to 15 m (50 ft) high. Like clove it is a native of the Molucca Islands and the history of this culinary herb is very similar, except that it reached Europe at an even later date — not until the 16th century. For this we can be grateful to the Arabian navigators of that day who not only knew how to sail safely across the Arabian Sea but also had the necessary commercial contacts in India and the Far East. The price of nutmeg was exorbitantly high and remained so until the 19th century, when, thanks to Christopher Smith, botanist and member of the East India Company, nutmeg began to be raised elsewhere and not only in the spice islands, as the Moluccas were called.

The fruits of the tree, one-seeded berries slightly resembling a peach, yield two spices: nutmeg and mace. Nutmeg (1) is the seed without the hard outer seed coat, whereas mace is the dried, fleshy, flat aril (2) which encloses the seed and extends beyond it in up to fifteen narrow strips. The fresh aril is a lovely red, changing to orange when it dries.

In the Middle Ages nutmeg was prized as a spice added not only to food but also to beer and used as a medicine to strengthen the stomach. Nowadays it is used as a flavouring for vegetables, salads and soups as well as breads and pastries. Mace, on the other hand, is used to flavour meat soups, sausages and salamis, vegetables and also in certain herb mixtures.

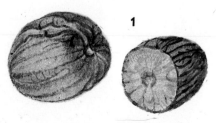

1

The nutmeg is dioecious and one male tree is planted to pollinate every 20 female trees. It produces flowers and fruits in succession throughout the year. A single tree yields as many as 2,000 fruits, which are gathered into baskets attached to long bamboo poles.

The chief commercial producers of both spices are Indonesia, Sri Lanka and southern and eastern India. Two sorts of nutmeg are available in the shops: East Indian, graded according to size, and West Indian, ungraded.

2

Myrtle
Myrtus communis

Anyone who has strolled along the narrow paths on the sun-baked stony hillsides along the Mediterranean coast will immediately recognize this fragrant evergreen shrub. Together with rosemary it forms the vegetation typical of this dry, sunny climate, filling the air with perfume.

The commonest use of myrtle as a seasoning is somewhat unusual: the freshly-cut twigs are added to the fire when spit-roasting whole sheep. The fragrant essential oil is liberated during the process and absorbed by the roasting meat. Fresh and dried leaves may be used also to season fatty meats, mainly roast pork. In Mediterranean countries it is customary to add myrtle to small roast birds, best of all just before serving, allowing a few minutes for the aroma to be absorbed.

Myrtle is a tender evergreen shrub. It is often grown in pots in the house, conservatory or on sheltered patios because of its ornamental flowers (1), glossy leaves and attractive habit. The flowers of shrubs growing in the wild are followed by many-seeded berries (2), which are green at first, later turning blue. Plants grown in pots, though they flower, rarely produce fruits. It is an old custom for guests at a wedding to wear a sprig of myrtle tied with a white ribbon on the lapel or shoulder and for brides to wear a wreath of myrtle on the head.

1

2

Watercress
Nasturtium officinale

Watercress is a perennial herb up to 80 cm (32 in) high. A native of Europe, it has become naturalized throughout the world, growing wild alongside brooks and streams in lowland country as well as in mountains. The young leaves have a pleasant taste resembling that of horseradish and are used, chiefly in Scandinavian countries, as a pungent salad rich in vitamins. Watercress was popular in the days of the Roman Empire. According to preserved records it was eaten in medieval France and Germany. Only the fresh young leaves are used. If you wish to keep them fresh for several days it is recommended to immerse the whole plant in cold water, cover the container with a lid and place it in a cool place. Otherwise it will grow, even in a vase of water, and lose its quality. Storing it in the refrigerator is not recommended.

Watercress is used to flavour salads and cheeses and as a garnish in canapés. It gives a pleasant taste to vegetable soups and goes well with freshwater fish. It can also be sprinkled, like chives, on boiled, buttered potatoes, omelettes and scrambled eggs. It is used to make herb butter, often mixed with other aromatic plants. In winter the ripe, ground seeds may be used instead of the leaves in the same ways, and also for flavouring stewed meat. It is advisable not to pick watercress growing wild for plants growing by contaminated water have been known to cause typhus in people that have eaten them. It is always safer to buy watercress for this has been carefully cultivated in uncontaminated water.

In western and central Europe not only
N. officinale can be found, but also the closely
related, small-leaved species
 N. microphyllum, which can be used in the
same way. In England nasturtium is the
common name for *Tropaeolum majus,*
cultivated for its brilliantly coloured flowers;
its seeds and leaves have a pungent flavour
similar to that of watercress.

Fennel Flower
Nigella sativa

Nigella sativa is a less attractive plant than the closely related *Nigella damascena* (Love-in-a-mist), often grown for garden decoration. However, it does yield black seeds resembling those of onion that have a bitter flavour at first but after a while taste like pepper. They are sold in shops as 'black caraway' and another English name for the plant is 'devil-in-the-bush'. Quite a different image is evoked by the name 'cheveux de Vénus' as it is called in France, where it is also known as 'quatre-épices'.

The seeds are used as flavouring mostly in Egypt, the Middle East and India, but also in European cookery. They are used much the same as black pepper, in addition to which they are added also to bread and baked foods. One advantage is that they do not irritate the lining of the stomach, but on the other hand they contain some substances that are poisonous. Therefore it is recommended to use them sparingly.

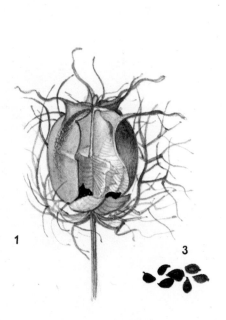

Fennel flower is an annual herb growing to a height of 40 cm (16 in) and flowering from spring until autumn. It is propagated by means of seeds sown early in spring in the open garden where the plants are to grow. The fruits, large decorative capsules (1, 2) divided into five compartments, are collected successively as they ripen. The seeds (3) are removed from the capsules after they have dried.

Sweet Basil
Ocimum basilicum

Lamiaceae

This aromatic herb is important not only in cookery but also as a medicinal plant and to bee-keepers, for it is often visited by bees. It derives its botanical name from the Greek words 'ozein', meaning to smell, and 'basileus', meaning king, because of its pleasant and penetrating aroma truly worthy of kings. Though native to southern Asia it has become established in the mountain ranges of tropical Asia and Africa and on the islands of the Pacific. In the mid-16th century it was introduced to Europe where it rapidly became and remained a popular culinary herb until it was relegated to the sidelines by the import of a wide assortment of oriental spices from the East. It made a comeback, however, during the Second World War, when spices were hard to come by. The fragrance of the foliage is due to the presence of an essential oil which is used also in the perfume industry. Fresh or dried leaves are used primarily for flavouring salads, in recipes where tomatoes are used (also ketchup), in fish as well as meat dishes (ragouts), sauces, sausages and salamis, raw vegetable dishes, herb butter, omelettes and turtle soup. It is very popular in Italian cookery.

A 15th-century manuscript lists it as one of several herbs that should be grown for flavouring soups. In the Middle Ages it is also found in recipes for pickling vegetables. Dioscorides, however, warned against eating too much basil, because it supposedly weakens the eyesight and is difficult to digest.

Sweet basil is an annual herb growing up to 40 cm (16 in) high. It is propagated only from seed. Ripe seeds remain viable for as long as five years. Because the plant is very sensitive to frost it is recommended to sow the seeds in open ground after all danger of frost is past. Fresh leaves are best for use as flavouring. It is not an easy herb to dry. The leaves must be dried very carefully in thin layers in a shaded, well-ventilated spot at a temperature not exceeding 35°C (95°F).

If moisture condenses on them or if they are
dried in direct sunlight over a long period
the leaves lose their pale-green colour. The
herb is harvested during the flowering
period; this may be done as often as three
times a year by leaving the bottom of the
leafy stem so the plant will put out new
shoots again. Flowers are produced from
June until late August.

141

Olive
Olea europaea

The existence of olives as food is the result of sheer chance combined with a stroke of genius. Present-day olive trees are apparently descended from a wild tree of Greek origin. The first such individual must have been the result of a chance mutation, some time as far back as 3,000 B.C., and all the olive trees raised nowadays are its offspring, multiplied by man.

In the first century B.C. the largest producer of olive oil was Italy, where the olive tree was introduced by the Greeks. Olives, as we know them today in the form used to flavour dishes typical of the Mediterranean region, were not known at that time. The reason is simple – the fresh fruits are inedible because of their unpleasant bitter flavour. This bitter flavour disappears only after lengthy immersion in water that is changed repeatedly, or after pickling in brine for several months. How and when this treatment was discovered we do not know, nor do we know whether our taste was enriched by chance or by man's ingenuity.

Pickled green olives are prepared from unripe fruits, black olives from ripe fruits. Both may be added to cold hors d'œuvres and salads, as well as to hot dishes, mainly to roast poultry, cooked vegetables and Italian pizza. Not only the pickled olives but also the fine oil obtained by pressing the ripe fruits is a flavouring. It is yellowish to greenish and has a very delicate flavour and aroma. Put a few drops on a salad of fresh green peppers or tomatoes, close your eyes, and it does not take much to imagine you are by the warm Mediterranean Sea. It is particularly good mixed with wine vinegar or lemon juice, but the addition of other herbs would only spoil the illusion.

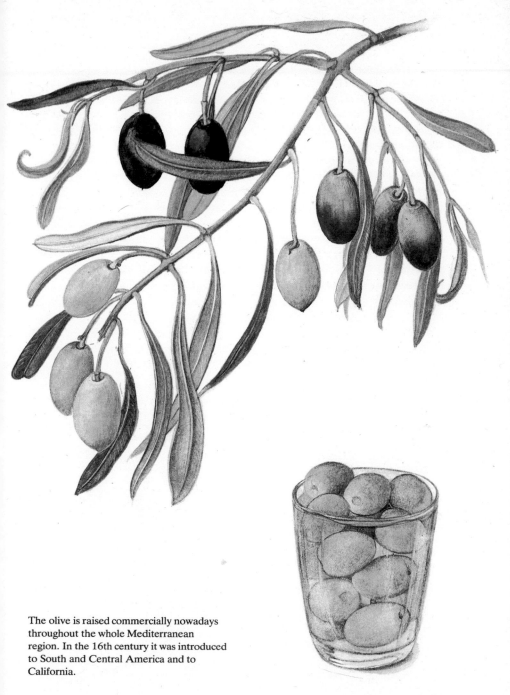

The olive is raised commercially nowadays throughout the whole Mediterranean region. In the 16th century it was introduced to South and Central America and to California.

Wild Marjoram, Oregano
Origanum vulgare

Lamiaceae

A Neapolitan pizza would be incomplete without oregano. This plant is native to the temperate and subtropical regions of Eurasia, but it grows wild as far north as central Scandinavia and the northern USSR as well as in North America. Most aromatic, however, are the plants that grow on the sunny limestone hillsides of southern Italy. No doubt this is the result not only of suitable soil and climate but also of natural selection which came up with the right variety, for this species includes a great many forms.

Though a traditional flavouring of Italian cookery, oregano is widely used throughout Europe and is commonly available in shops. It is one of the most widely-used seasonings in Mexico, perhaps because it grows wild there too. It is generally used dried, even though the fresh herb has a more penetrating flavour. It is very good together with tomatoes, cheese, vegetables (especially beans), meat and fish.

Oregano is not only an excellent culinary herb but also a popular perennial plant grown for decoration in the garden where it makes flowering, solitary specimens up to 50 cm (20 in) high. It does best in a warm, dry location with limestone substrate, otherwise it has no special requirements. It is readily propagated from seeds sown into boxes in early spring, also by the division of older clumps.

For winter use cut the flowering
top parts, tie in bunches and hang
in a well-ventilated spot to dry. When quite
dry discard thicker stalks, rub rest of plant
between the hands and store in closed, dry
jars.

Oregano has medicinal properties too, for
it aids digestion. It is also important to
bee-keepers as it is much visited by bees.

145

Opium Poppy
Papaver somniferum

There are many species of wild poppies but the opium poppy has never been found growing in the wild. In all probability it was bred from the wild species *P. setigerum,* native to the Mediterranean region. It is a useful plant for many reasons. The pharmaceutical industry processes the juice (opium) which exudes from cuts on the unripe capsules, and obtains morphine and many other opium alkaloids from the empty, dry capsules. The ripe seeds yield the edible oil called 'olivette' by the French and a lower quality industrial oil used in synthetic dyes.

In cookery the ripe seeds are used to make poppy-seed cakes and fillings for pastries. Cooking and baking makes their pleasant, nut-like flavour more pronounced. Poppy-seeds are also sprinkled on rolls and buns. Ground seeds are added to pungent herb mixtures not only for their flavour but also to improve the consistency and increase the weight of the mixtures. This is much better than diluting them with starchy flour, as is often done by European producers.

The type species from which the currently cultivated varieties are derived was already grown in Europe and Asia Minor for its oily seeds in the Stone Age. The opium poppy made its appearance in the first century A.D. and its cultivation, this time for its narcotic effects, rapidly spread to Italy, Egypt and Arabia, and later in the 9th century farther east to Iran, India and China.

Nowadays its cultivation is officially restricted (for fear of its misuse as a narcotic) but the seeds remain a sought-after culinary ingredient. The capsules must be allowed to ripen thoroughly before harvesting, for the unripe seeds have the same effect as opium.

Parsley
Petroselinum crispum

Daucaceae

In ancient Greece parsley was believed to be sacred and the symbol of fame and joy. It could not possibly be used for such a plebeian purpose as food when it adorned the head of the great Heracles on ceremonial occasions. This belief fell into oblivion but the custom of using it as decoration has been retained to this day, albeit in somewhat different form. The fresh leaves of the curly variety are used to decorate window displays by butchers and fishmongers. Parsley did not become a culinary herb until the Middle Ages when Charlemagne had it raised in his vegetable gardens, after which it rapidly became an essential part of all vegetable dishes. It reached England in the 16th century and was brought to America by the settlers.

Its delicate aroma and flavour have made parsley the most widely-used culinary herb which can be added to practically all dishes that are not sweet. The finely chopped leaves are used either fresh or dried. It can be combined well with other kitchen herbs. Crushed parsley seeds may be used for flavouring instead of the leaves, though this is not a common practice. Parsley leaves are an important component of bouquet garni and a common ingredient of a great variety of commercial sauces.

Parsley is a biennial herb native to the Mediterranean region. It is propagated by seeds that germinate several weeks after sowing. A leafy rosette is formed in the first year; this may be picked from June until winter. The second year it produces a flowering stem up to 1 m (3 ft) high and after the seeds have ripened it dies.

Two types are cultivated: the one for its curly leaves, used for flavouring and as a garnish, the other for its fleshy root, commonly used as a vegetable. In the autumn the plants may be put in pots, thus ensuring a continual supply of fresh leaves, rich in Vitamin C, throughout the winter. As cooking destroys vitamins it is recommended to add the chopped leaves just before serving.

149

Allspice, Pimento
Pimenta officinalis

Myrtaceae

Surprisingly allspice, one of the best-known tropical spices found in the kitchen of every home, is the latest to be introduced to Europe. It was known to the Aztecs of Mexico a long time ago but Europe did not learn of it till Christopher Columbus made his famous voyage of discovery. Even then Europeans did not begin using it until the turn of the 17th and 18th century. It has been known longest in England, where it is called allspice because its flavour resembles a mixture of pepper, clove and cinnamon.

Whole dried fruits (berries) are used to flavour roast meats, mainly game, and in marinades of all kinds; ground berries are used in rice, pâtés, soups and sauces. Allspice is used widely in making sausages as well as liqueurs such as Benedictine and Chartreuse. The essential oil is used by the perfume industry.

The tree is evergreen and grows up to 13 m (43 ft) high. It has large aromatic leaves up to 10 cm (4 in) long and equally aromatic bark that peels off regularly every year. The small whitish flowers (1) are arranged in terminal clusters (2). The berries (3, 4) are divided into two chambers with one seed (5) in each. When ripe they are coloured red and lose their aroma. They are therefore harvested while still green, being picked by hand and dried in the sun.

2

1

The smooth berries become wrinkled as they dry. A single grown-up tree yields up to 40 kg (90 lb) of dry berries a year. The best allspice comes from Jamaica; it is also raised in Guatemala, Honduras and Brazil. Mexican allspice has larger fruits but they are less aromatic.

Anise
Pimpinella anisum

Anise is an annual herb native to the eastern Mediterranean region (Egypt, Asia Minor, the Greek islands). In ancient times it was used mostly as a medicine to treat snake bites, nightmares and the like. The ancient Greeks introduced it to the Romans who also began using it in cookery. It was not until the 14th century, however, that it reached Europe as a flavouring for bread − aniseed bread is popular to this day, particularly in Austria and southern Germany. Nowadays anise is grown commercially on a large scale in Bulgaria, Italy, Spain, France, the USSR, Turkey, Mexico and elsewhere.

Used as a flavouring are the fragrant, small, hard, greyish-brown, double achenes which have a pleasant sweetish taste. The aroma is due to the presence of an essential oil containing anethol. It is used as a cough medicine, in lozenges, and in flavouring liqueurs, most typical being anisette. Anise is a characteristic flavouring for sweet dishes, cookies and coffee-cakes. It is also added to plum preserves and to pickled gherkins.

In the Middle Ages anise was a highly prized and costly spice. It is mentioned along with fennel, coriander and caraway, in complicated recipes for making preserves of nuts, honey and raisins. It was also sprinkled, together with bay leaf, on pig's-foot jelly.

Nowadays anise has become established in the wild in Europe and Asia, as well as in North America. Principal producers are Bulgaria, Italy, Spain, France, the USSR, Turkey and Mexico.

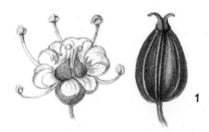

1

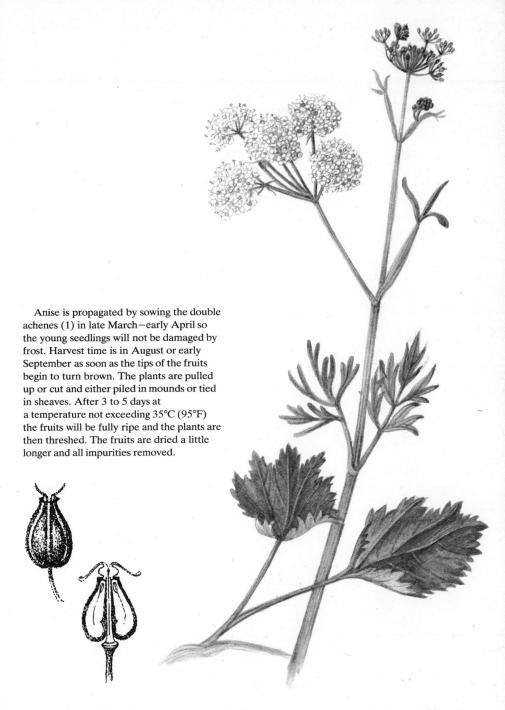

Anise is propagated by sowing the double achenes (1) in late March—early April so the young seedlings will not be damaged by frost. Harvest time is in August or early September as soon as the tips of the fruits begin to turn brown. The plants are pulled up or cut and either piled in mounds or tied in sheaves. After 3 to 5 days at a temperature not exceeding 35°C (95°F) the fruits will be fully ripe and the plants are then threshed. The fruits are dried a little longer and all impurities removed.

Burnet Saxifrage
Pimpinella saxifraga

Burnet saxifrage is a perennial herb up to 60 cm (2 ft) high that was used in cookery long ago but not very often nowadays. The botanical name for the genus is a corrupted version of the Latin word 'bipinella' referring to the twice-pinnate leaves. It was already known to the ancient Greeks, who called it 'kaukalis'. It is used to this day as a medicinal plant for its diuretic as well as digestive and expectorant properties. In the Middle Ages it was believed to ward off the plague.

The delicately-scented, mildly pungent leaves with a cucumber-like flavour are used for flavouring. These are eaten as a salad by southern Europeans, the same as the leaves of burnet *(Sanguisorba minor)*. The young basal leaves are the tastiest if picked before the flower stem begins to grow. They are used only fresh to flavour salads, vegetable soups and sauces. They may also be used as a garnish for cold-dishes. They are particularly good as an ingredient of fine herb mixtures, for flavouring mayonnaises, boiled vegetables and fish. They may be used together with chervil, tarragon, parsley, chives and the like.

Burnet saxifrage grows wild throughout nearly the whole of Europe and the Middle East. It is commonly found on dry banks, in meadows, by the wayside and on the edge of forests. If you want fresh foliage the whole summer long, however, you can grow it in the garden, windowbox or simply In a pot. All it needs is a sunny location and not too much moisture. It may be propagated by means of seeds (achenes), or by the division of older clumps.

155

Black Pepper

Piper nigrum

The coastal region in south-west India known as the Malabar Coast was originally called Malichabar. The name is derived from the Sanskrit word 'malicha', meaning pepper and the Arabian word 'bar', meaning land, hence pepper land. This relatively narrow coastal belt is the original home of the pepper plant, a climbing shrub growing to a height of 6 m (20 ft). Pepper is a typical plant of the tropics that thrives only in a very humid and warm climate. Originally a forest plant grown by the natives to climb among trees at the edge of the forest, it is now widely cultivated throughout the tropics. It is raised on plantations from offshoots that climb up poles up to 4 m (13 ft) high. Newly planted plants do not begin to bear fruit until the third year and produce their maximum yields (up to 3.5 kg [8 lb] of berries on a single plant) at the age of 7 to 9 years. The berries are harvested before they ripen when they are still green or yellow (they are red when ripe) – this is done over a period of several months as the berries ripen in succession.

Pepper is the most widely consumed of all seasonings because of its many uses not only in the kitchen but also at the table (no table is properly set without salt and pepper). It is used either whole or ground, by itself or in a wide variety of mixtures for flavouring meat, sausages, fish, soups, sauces, vegetables, salads and so on.

The unripe berries (1) are dried in the sun, during which process they become black and wrinkled (2), and then graded according to size; this is the black pepper of commerce. Fruits that have ripened on the plant (3) are soaked in water for 2 to 3 days after they are picked; this softens the fleshy covering which can then be easily removed. The cleaned, husked, ripe seeds yield the white pepper (4) of commerce, which is more aromatic but not as pungent. Unripe green pepper steeped in vinegar and salt has a very delicate aroma.

1

2

3

4

157

Pepper Cubeb
Piper cubeba

This is a climbing perennial plant native to the islands of Java, Sumatra and Borneo. It is grown on trees which shade plantations of other plants from the tropical sun.

Of all the peppers used in cookery this is the most aromatic, which accounts, perhaps, for its lack of popularity in Europe. The only peoples that use it are those living in warmer climates (it is used in the same way as black pepper). In the past it was more highly prized and much more in demand than nowadays. It was used in India as a folk medicine before the Christian era and it was the Indians who introduced it to the Arabs, who called it Indian spice. Venetian merchants brought it to Europe, where it was a popular spice for centuries. In the 19th century, when English officers in Java discovered that the natives used it to treat inflammation of the urinary passages, it was also included in the list of Europe's pharmaceutics.

Besides being far more pungent, pepper cubeb is also morphologically different from black pepper and long pepper. Though the fruits (berries) resemble those of black pepper they appear to have long stalks (these stalks are actually elongated ovaries). They are harvested before they ripen so that the surface becomes wrinkled during the drying process. The strong biting quality of cubeb is not caused by piperine, as in black pepper, but by cubebine and by the large amount of essential oil they contain (as much as 12% whereas black pepper contains 4% at the most). The specific composition of the essential oil together with the resin present in the spice gives pepper cubeb its characteristic camphor-like aroma.

159

Long Pepper
Piper longum

Piperaceae

The spice known as long pepper is obtained from two species of plants: one is *Piper longum* from India and the other is *Piper officinarum* from the Sunda Islands, Philippines and Moluccas. In both instances the dried unripe berries are used as seasoning. They are more pungent than black pepper and, unlike black pepper, form joined, compact fruits resembling hard, black catkins up to 5 cm (2 in) long.

The first to know and use long pepper, apart from the natives, were the Persians, followed by the Greeks, who called it 'péperi', or rather 'péperi makrón', meaning large pepper, in order to distinguish it from black pepper. The Romans, who were introduced to it by the ancient Greeks, changed the name péperi to piper and called it *Piper longum*. The Latin word 'piper' then gave rise to the common names used in the various European languages, e. g. pepper, Pfeffer, poivre. Long pepper played a remarkably important role in European trade in the Middle Ages. The name 'piperarii', a medieval term applied to successful merchants, was used in this sense up until modern times. Nowadays, however, long pepper is cultivated and used mostly in India, the Far East and the Pacific region. Indians add it to curry and to a mixture called pipel.

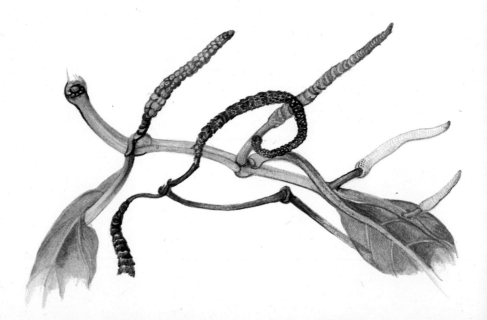

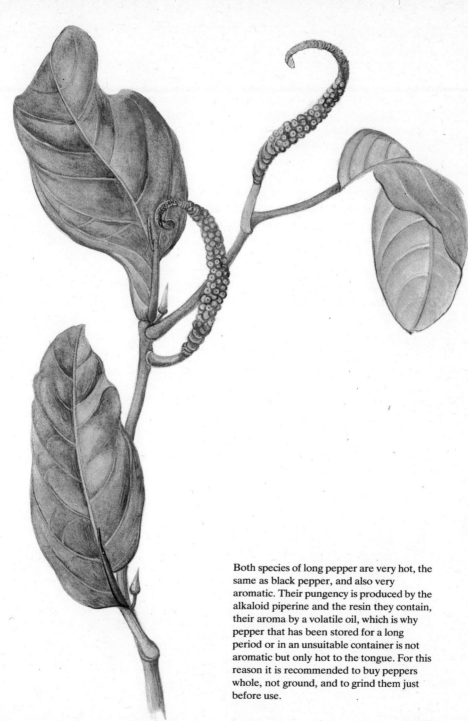

Both species of long pepper are very hot, the
same as black pepper, and also very
aromatic. Their pungency is produced by the
alkaloid piperine and the resin they contain,
their aroma by a volatile oil, which is why
pepper that has been stored for a long
period or in an unsuitable container is not
aromatic but only hot to the tongue. For this
reason it is recommended to buy peppers
whole, not ground, and to grind them just
before use.

161

Purslane
Portulaca oleracea

Portulacaceae

Purslane is native to India and Pakistan where it grows wild and where it was being eaten a thousand years ago. Nowadays it occurs as a weed of fields in the warmer parts of central Europe as well as in North and South America. It is often grown in gardens and is raised on a larger scale in the Middle East and central Europe.

In the Middle Ages it was a very popular plant in Europe, particularly in England during the reign of Elizabeth I. Its uses are many. The fleshy leaves may be cooked and eaten like spinach. In France it is used to make an excellent, vitamin-rich, green salad and in the Middle East it is a common ingredient of mixed salads called 'fattoush'. According to old English recipes the leaves may be pickled like capers. They may be used as a delicate flavouring in creamed vegetable soups and in piquant mayonnaises served with meat and fish. When using purslane in cooked foods the finely chopped leaves should be added at the end of cooking to retain their delicate flavour and precious vitamins.

Purslane is an annual herb with fleshy stems and leaves. There are two forms: the subspecies *P. o. sylvestris* (1) which has a prostrate stem and the cultivated form. *P. o. sativa* (2) which is generally erect, up to 60 cm (2 ft) high and much more fleshy

1

162

Purslane is well known for its easy cultivation. It is propagated by seed sown outdoors in a sunny location where the plants are to grow. Growth is rapid. The first young leaves may be picked within a month and then at regular intervals until the flowering period.

2

Radish
Raphanus sativus radicula

Brassicaceae

The ancient Chinese dictionary *Er-ya* tells us that radishes were already being grown in China in the middle of the second millenium B.C. The wild species are native to that land and the number of Chinese varieties is enormous. Even older, by a thousand years, are the inscriptions on a tablet of the Great Pyramid of Cheops, where the radish (surmaia) is listed together with various other vegetables. Either it was introduced from here to China or else the Chinese began cultivating it on their own, independent of the Egyptians. Radish is also mentioned by Dioscorides in connection with its use in medicine.

Until recently there was no doubt that the predecessor of the present-day radish was *Raphanus sativus,* the oldest wild species of the genus, but now many authorities are proving that today's radishes are derived from another wild species of the same genus, namely *R. raphanistrum.* Be it as it may, the present selection of radishes includes many forms differing in size, colour and shape. All, however, have a pleasant flavour, pungent in some and less so in others, for which reason they are classed as a seasoning. They are used sliced on bread and butter, chopped or grated in salads and as an accompaniment to cheeses and salamis. They are best eaten raw. Radishes are wholesome, for besides mustard oil they contain Vitamins B and C and many mineral substances.

The radish is a rapidly growing annual herb. The seeds germinate as soon as they are sown and in congenial conditions the radishes are ready for consumption within three weeks. However, they should be thinned to the proper spacing (about 4 cm [1 1/2 in] apart), because plants that are too crowded tend to grow tall and flower (1) instead of forming a fleshy root. The same happens when radishes are sown in summer (they usually run to seed), which is why they should be grown in a shaded spot at that time of the year. The slower and longer their growth, the drier they become and the hotter their taste.

1

Sumach
Rhus coriaria

Sumach is a shrub up to 3 m (10 ft) high growing wild in the Mediterranean region and southeast Asia on stony banks high up above the seashore. It is grown for its sour fruits (1) in southern Italy and Sicily. In Lebanon it may be seen in front of almost every house, the fruits being dried and ground into a purplish-red powder, or soaked in water and the juice then pressed out. They have a sour and pleasantly astringent taste. The fruits were used by the ancient Romans, who called the plant Syrian sumach, for the same purpose as lemons before the latter were introduced into cultivation. From Mattioli we learn that the eastern peoples used the dried fruits of sumach in place of salt.

The red powder may be purchased in shops that specialize in foodstuffs from Lebanon, but it is rarely used in Europe. However, sumach is very important in Arabian cookery, where it is still preferred to lemon. The juice is used to flavour salads and the powder in various dishes, mainly fish. It may also be used with stewed poultry, vegetables and roast meat. Because of its high tannin content sumach is a suitable ingredient in fatty foods, promoting digestion and checking diarrhoea.

Some species of sumach are grown for the tannin-rich leaves used in tanning and dyeing. The related stag's horn sumach *(R. typhina)* (2) is often grown in Europe as a specimen tree. This is native to North America, the home of many poisonous species such as *R. toxicodendron,* commonly known as poison ivy.

Dog Rose
Rosa canina

In the Middle Ages the rose was called the 'flower of flowers' and from that time dates the recipe for the then popular dish called 'Rosée'. This consisted of a capon perfumed with rose petals and flavoured with almonds, sugar and saffron. In society rose sugar was a favoured sweetener and rose water was used to rinse the fingers at banquets. Syrup prepared by mixing honey and rose petals was prescribed for 'the weak, ill, phlegmatic, melancholic and choleric'. To this day rose petals are used locally, particularly in the Near East, as a fragrant admixture to foods and beverages.

The fruits − rose hips, rich in Vitamin C, are used to make a refreshing, slightly sour tea and very piquant marmalade, good by itself as well as added to sauces and roast game. The fleshy hips contain a great many hard, pointed-ovate achenes covered with silky hairs. These must be removed before using the hips in cookery. It is a very tedious task consisting of cutting each hip lenghtwise while still fresh and scraping out the contents. It is a lengthy and unpleasant process, best done with gloved hands, for the hairs cause an itching sensation if they come in contact with the skin. Hips for making jam, marmalade and wine must be fully ripe and picked when they have become softened after the first frosts.

The dog rose is widely distributed throughout Europe up to altitudes of 1,000 m (3,300 ft) and therefore there is no need to grow it in the garden. It may be found alongside hedges in pastures, on sunny banks and at the edges of woodlands. It is perennial, growing up to 3 m (10 ft) high, and fully hardy. It was named *Rosa canina* from the Latin word 'canis' meaning dog because the root was at one time used to treat rabies. Nowadays the hips are used by the pharmaceutical industry primarily as a source of Vitamin C. The hips of the ramanas rose *(Rosa rugosa)*, which are much larger, are used for the same purposes.

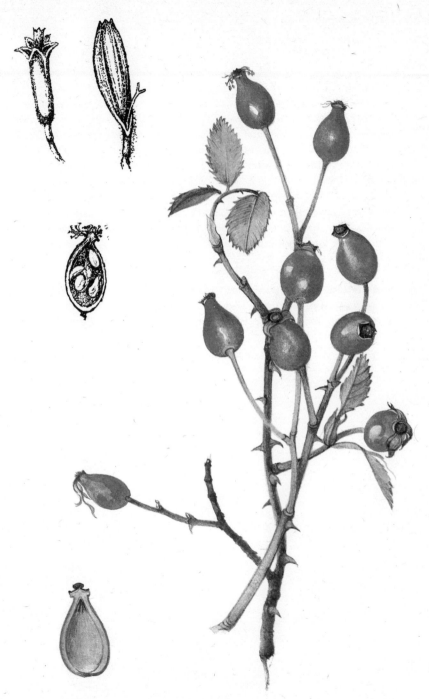

169

Rosemary
Rosmarinus officinalis

Lamiaceae

The popularity of rosemary in antiquity and the Middle Ages cannot be matched by any other plant. It was dedicated to the goddess Venus. The Romans adorned the heads of their household gods with rosemary garlands and this ancient custom was carried over into medieval times, but in a different form — the boar's head was always decked with a wreath of rosemary at the Christmas feast. In those days this plant was the subject of many superstitions — it was believed to have the power of making a person merry, happy and gay, of banishing nightmares and of preserving youth. In cookery it was used as a seasoning in salads and in sauces for fish dishes, also for flavouring wine. Medieval housewives placed it in their wardrobes and bookcases as a moth deterrent. Its many uses make rosemary an important addition to every garden.

As a seasoning it is most popular in Italy, France and England, where it is used with meat, mainly mutton, pork and game, as well as poultry, fish, in sauces, soups, salads and pickled vegetables. It is used crushed or ground and added to foods when they are almost ready to eat, for lengthy cooking would cause evaporation of the essential oil that gives it its fragrance. Rosemary is an excellent seasoning but must be used sparingly, for larger doses may be deleterious.

Rosemary is an evergreen shrub reaching
a height of 2 m (6 ft). It is native to the
Mediterranean region. It is readily damaged
by frost so should be planted in a sheltered
position in the garden. It can be grown in
pots and put indoors in a light, cool room or
conservatory for the winter. The pleasantly
sweet, camphor-like fragrance of the foliage
is produced by the presence of a large
amount of essential oil (up to 2%) and resin.
For flavouring it is best to use fresh leaves; if
they are dried this must be done at
a temperature not exceeding 35°C (95°F).
The leaves should be picked during and
after the flowering period, for that is when
they are most aromatic.

Rosemary is grown primarily for its
fragrant essential oil, used in making
shampoo, soap, and toilet water. It is raised
for this purpose not only in southern Europe
but also in North Africa, England and the
USSR.

Rue
Ruta graveolens

The flavouring and medicinal properties of rue were known to the Romans who introduced it to the rest of Europe (the scientific name is derived from the Greek word 'rhyesthai', meaning to save or to help). The blue-green foliage as well as the seeds were used, not only to flavour salads, vegetable omelettes and sauces served with fish, but also to treat various diseases. It was used as an antidote against poisons and to banish evil spirits. An unknown writer of the 6th century B.C. recommends: 'for the malady called lethargy, which is forgetfulness, take the herb rue, rinse it in vinegar and lay it on the brow'. In the Middle Ages it was used in making herb wines, hence the German name Weinraute.

The fresh tender leaves or dry powdered leaves are used for flavouring. Their bitter properties stimulate the appetite and the unusual aroma gives a pleasant taste mainly to fish, eggs and cheese spreads. This herb takes getting used to, for many people do not like it at first. It is used in combination with other herbs in cooking game. Rue should be added to foods just before the end of cooking time and in very small amounts, for large doses are toxic. In persons with sensitive skin it causes a painful rash. In southern Europe, shoots of the plant are used to give aroma to the brandy called grappa. It may also be recommended as flavouring for vegetable juice cocktails and in making aromatic vinegars.

Rue is a perennial, evergreen bushy sub-shrub. Native to the eastern Mediterranean region, it grows wild in southern Europe and the Middle East, where it thrives on well-drained soils in sunny locations. The greenish-yellow flowers (1) are followed by green, lobed capsules (2). It is easy to grow in the garden, being propagated either by seed or by cuttings. Frequent cutting back of the non-woody parts will promote growth of lush foliage. The top parts should be dried at a temperature of less than 35°C (95°F), a process that takes as long as 8 days, and the leaves then stripped from the stems.

Common Sage
Salvia officinalis

Lamiaceae

The scientific name of this plant is a pleonasm because the generic name *Salvia* is derived from the Latin word 'salvare', meaning to cure, and the specific name *officinalis* from the neo-Latin word 'officina,' meaning pharmacy. Despite the fact that sage is an important medicinal plant used by the Romans of ancient times, it also has its place in cookery. When and how it spread through Europe is not known, but one thing is certain — that it ranked high on the list of culinary herbs in the Middle Ages. 'How can a man die who has a sage in his garden' was a common Arabian saying. Recipes for pork in sage sauce and chicken with sage survive from that time. Sage was used in combination with ginger and bay leaf to flavour wine and by itself in preparing water for washing the hands at the table during banquets.

The fresh or dried leaves are used as a flavouring. The dried leaves can be either crushed or powdered. It is interesting to note the different ways sage is used by various nationalities. In the United States it is one of the most important seasonings for pork and sausage dishes, cheese dishes and baked fish. In England it is a classic ingredient of stuffing for duck and goose. The Dutch warm themselves with a hot drink of sage and milk when ice-skating in winter. Sage leaves dipped in batter and fried are commonly eaten in Switzerland, the Tyrol and upper Italy; these are called 'mice' because the long leaf-stalks sticking out of the batter resemble mouse tails.

Sage is a Mediterranean sub-shrub, native to the area extending from Dalmatia to Macedonia. The best quality sage is from the Yugoslav coast where it covers slopes up to altitudes of 1,800 m (5,760 ft). There are many varieties of sage grown on the Continent and in America. Propagation is by seed, sown in early spring or late autumn.

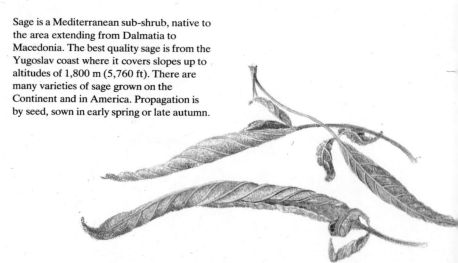

The foliage should be harvested shortly
before flowering and only in dry weather; it
should be dried at a temperature not
exceeding 35°C (95°F). The aroma of sage
is due to the presence of an essential oil,
tannins and bitter principles.

Clary
Salvia sclarea

Clary, a close relative of common sage, is native to southern Europe. The specific name is derived from the Latin word 'clarus', meaning clear, bright. It is a biennial with large leaves and tall stems up to 1 m (3 ft) high, and a good plant for the herb garden because it is hardy and the leaves may be used throughout the winter when fresh herbs are scarce.

In the Middle Ages it was called 'Oculus Christi', meaning the eye of Christ, and was added to vegetables and to meat dishes to give them a subtler taste. The famous French book *Le ménagier de Paris* includes it among the herbs for flavouring vegetable omelettes and in a recipe for a green marinade for preserving fish. In a 15th-century manuscript we find it listed amongst herbs and somewhat later we learn that 'some brewmasters add it to their beer to make it more intoxicating and thus please drunkards'. The seeds of clary were believed to counter 'eye weakness'.

The leaves are very aromatic and may be used both fresh and dried. They are added, together with the flowers of elderberry, to wine to give it a nutmeg-like flavour, hence the German name Muskateller-Salbei. They are also used to flavour jams and jellies.

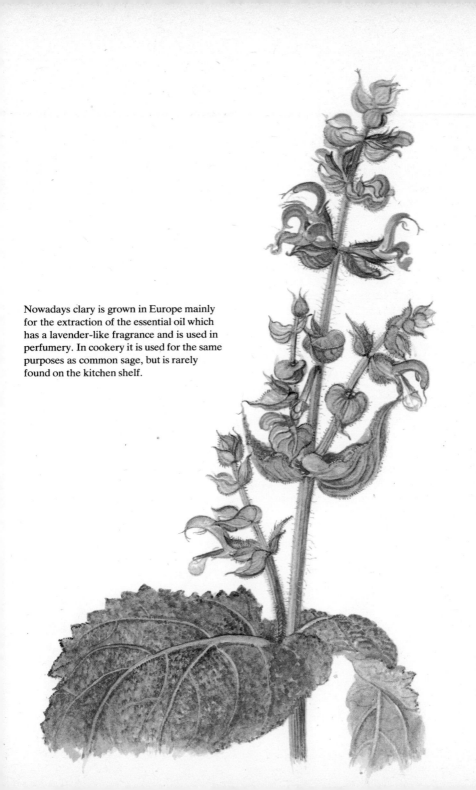

Nowadays clary is grown in Europe mainly for the extraction of the essential oil which has a lavender-like fragrance and is used in perfumery. In cookery it is used for the same purposes as common sage, but is rarely found on the kitchen shelf.

Elderberry
Sambucus nigra

Caprifoliaceae

The elderberry is a shrub up to 7 m (23 ft) high distributed throughout Europe, western Asia and North America. The white flowers, appearing in late spring – early summer, are followed by black fruits (*nigra* in Latin means black) – three-seeded berries, or rather drupes. The berries contain a deep red juice, hence the name *Sambucus,* derived from the Greek word 'sambyx', meaning red colour. Both the flowers and fruits are used in cookery.

The inflorescences are cut off as soon as they open, spread out on nets to wilt, the blooms are then stripped from the stalks and rapidly dried so they do not discolour. Dried blooms should be stored in air-tight containers. During the growth period it is best to use the fresh flowers. These have a refreshing fragrance and for this reason were at one time used in Europe to improve the flavour of Moselle wines that were not up to par. Nowadays they are used to flavour compotes, jellies and jams. They may also be added to flaky pastry. The flowers or extracts prepared from the flowers are also used by the pharmaceutical industry in medicines that stimulate secretion of the sweat glands.

The berries have a strong flavour and are used to make jams and juices rich in Vitamin C.

Their chief attraction in cookery is their lovely red colour which dissolves well in water. In former times elderberries were used to colour wine, chiefly port. They are added in small amounts to apple and pear compotes. In some north European countries they are used to make a fruit soup, eaten with baked apples and dumplings or toasted bread. They are also the principal ingredient of an old English ketchup called poulac.

The old branches of elderberry bushes are sometimes attacked by the fungus *Hirneola auricula-judae* – a popular food in China and Japan.

179

Burnet
Sanguisorba minor

Rosaceae

The scientific name of this plant is derived from that of the closely related *Sanguisorba officinalis,* whose roots are used in pharmaceutic preparations to check bleeding ('sanguis' is the Latin word for blood and 'sorbere' the Latin word meaning to absorb). In the case of *S. minor,* the leaves are used in cookery. They are a classic ingredient of herb butter and herb sauces such as ravigote and chivry. They are used fresh and finely chopped, but may be stored in the freezer. Tender young leaves are used to make an excellent salad called burnet salad, older leaves are too tough for this purpose. In Elizabethan England burnet was one of the basic herbs of the kitchen garden and it was from there that it was introduced to America by the first settlers. It is also very good for making herb vinegar, prepared, according to old recipes, by steeping the crushed seeds in wine vinegar. It may also be used the same as borage to flavour cold fruit cups. Nowadays it is used most in France and Italy.

1

Burnet is a perennial herb that usually dies back in winter. It has odd-pinnate leaves (1) for which reason it is often mistakenly classified as *Pimpinella*. The flowers are arranged in round clusters at the tips of upright stems. Propagation is by means of seeds or by the division of older clumps.

Summer Savory

Satureja hortensis

Caught up in the fast pace of the present day we often forget age-old culinary treats that made life pleasant for our ancestors. One of the most aromatic is the inconspicuous savory, recommended by Vergil to his countrymen. The Romans made a savory sauce rather like we now make mint sauce. Savory is native to the Mediterranean region; in the 9th century A.D. it was introduced to central Europe, where it rapidly became established. It was widely used for seasoning in the days when costly spices imported from the tropics were rare. In Germany it is used mostly to flavour beans (hence the name Bohnenkraut) and in English and French cookery in stuffing for turkey and roast veal. It is also good with fish and pickled vegetables. The youngest terminal leaflets have the most delicate aroma and are delicious in salads. Savory is also used to flavour sausage meat.

In the Middle Ages roast goose called 'Suce Madame' was prepared according to the following recipe: 'Take sage, parsley, hyssop and savory, quince and pears and stuff the goose, then close the cavity and sew it so the fat cannot escape, and roast it well'. Savory, however, had to be used sparingly for, as Mattioli wrote in his herbal, 'it incites to wantonness'. Mattioli derived its generic name from the satyrs of antiquity.

Summer savory is treated as an annual herb up to 30 cm (1 ft) high with stem that becomes woody at the base and branches like a shrub. The linear-lanceolate, short-stalked leaves are dotted on both sides with glands. The flowering period is from July until the frost; the fruits are nutlets.

It is very suitable for growing in the herb garden. Propagation is by means of seeds sown outdoors where the plants are to grow in early spring. The non-woody flowering top parts of the plant are gathered. These are tied in bunches and dried in a well-ventilated spot at a temperature not exceeding 35°C (95°F). They should then be stored in air-tight containers.

White Mustard
Sinapis alba

Brassicaceae

White mustard has long been cultivated. Native to the Mediterranean region, probably north Africa, its many present cultivated varieties differ only slightly from the original wild forms. It was cultivated by the ancient Greeks, Romans and Egyptians. From the writings of Theophrastus we learn that the Greeks called it 'napy' or also 'sinapi', which gave rise to the Latin name of the genus and later also to the German name Senf. Already in those days it was made into a paste for use as a condiment according to recipes quite different from those of the present day. The Romans introduced the plant and their recipes for prepared mustard to central and western Europe. In the Middle Ages wine vinegar, called 'mustum' in Latin, began to be used in making the paste and hence the North German name Mostrich, the French moutarde and the English mustard.

The seeds are used whole in pickling gherkins and vegetables, in making marinades and like coriander to flavour sausage meat. In England young seedlings are added to green salads. They may be grown readily and rapidly at home from seeds sown in a dish covered with a piece of damp flannel, where they will produce seedlings ready for picking within a week.

Nowadays white mustard is raised practically throughout the whole of Europe, in parts of the USSR and on a lesser scale in western Canada.

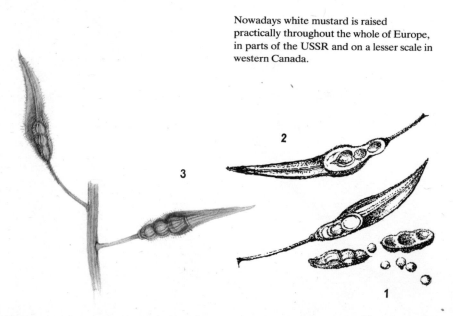

An annual herb reaching a height of 80 cm (32 in), it is readily distinguished from other mustards by the seeds (1) which are contained in pods (siliques) terminated by a prominent beak (2,3). They are straw-yellow in colour and are larger than other mustard seeds. Mustard has a brief growth period and ripening and harvesting depend on the time of sowing. It is harvested when the pods turn brownish-yellow and the seeds harden.

Mountain Ash, Rowan
Sorbus aucuparia

Rosaceae

Everyone knows this ornamental tree whose masses of white blooms decorate the countryside in early spring, followed in autumn by bright red berries which children string into beads. As a flavouring, however, rowan-berries continue to be neglected. Perhaps because in this overly-civilized world where we can purchase everything packaged and ready-made we have forgotten to look about us and make the most of nature's bounty, of the fruits which are not found on the market but are plentiful in the wild. Rowanberries are subtly piquant fruits reminiscent of cranberries with their slightly bitter, aromatic flavour and bright colouring. Forms with sweet fruits are ideal not only for making compotes, jams and wines, but above all for flavouring roast beef, roast game and cream sauces, to which, besides taste and aroma, they also give a lovely colour. Rowanberries furthermore have excellent setting properties due to their high pectin content. They are therefore used to make jellies that are an excellent accompaniment to meat and fish dishes. The berries may also be dried without any loss in quality.

The rowan is distributed throughout western and central Europe from the lowlands up to the tree-line and in northern Europe, even north of the Arctic Circle. It is a small, deciduous, rapidly-growing tree reaching a maximum height of 20 m (65 ft); it is not very long-lived and its wood is of little value. Its one advantage is that it is completely hardy. The fruits are eaten by birds, chiefly starlings and blackbirds, a fact made use of by fowlers who used to capture them on the tree; the Latin name of the species is derived from 'avis capere', meaning to catch birds. The rowan is not harmed by the birds; on the contrary, it benefits because the birds disperse the seeds, which they cannot digest and thus pass out with their faeces, thereby spreading the species.

187

Tansy
Tanacetum vulgare

Compositae/Asteraceae

Tansy, a perennial herb up to 1 m (3 ft) high, is native to Europe where it is widely distributed. Its Latin name is derived from the Greek word 'athanasia', meaning immortality. It was very popular in the Middle Ages. Tansy was grown in the herb garden of Charlemagne, and in England it was widely used as a medicinal herb in the days of Elizabeth I. The tender young leaves combined with eggs were a popular dish called 'tansy', eaten at Easter to celebrate the end of fasting. This custom has survived to this day in the form of Easter cakes and puddings flavoured with tansy leaves. It was also believed to banish 'bad humours' caused by a lengthy diet of salt fish. The highly aromatic, rather unpleasant-tasting foliage was used to disguise the strong taste of game and mutton and make it more palatable.

Nowadays tansy is a flavouring that is fast disappearing from cookery, and if used, then generally as an interesting and unusual ingredient. Gourmets recommend using the leaves in omelettes, stuffings, fish dishes and salads, but always sparingly, for larger amounts are toxic. Only young, freshly-picked leaves are used.

Tansy may still occasionally be encountered in gardens, where it is generally grown for decoration. The ornamental form *T. vulgare crispum* is often cultivated. The yellow, button-like flower-heads are composed only of tubular flowers (1); female flowers round the perimeter and bisexual flowers in the centre.

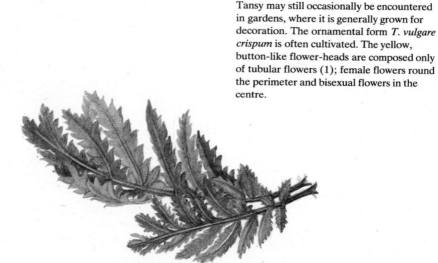

1

Cocoa
Theobroma cacao

Byttneriaceae

Cocoa, or more correctly cacao, is a small evergreen tree native to tropical America, probably originally growing in the Orinoco River basin. Linné (Linnaeus) gave it the lovely name *Theobroma,* meaning food of the Gods. Its occurrence in the wild as well as its cultivation is restricted to the inland tropics with their heavy rainfall and rich soil. Over the years growers have bred and developed a great variety of cultivated forms and we no longer know what the original wild trees were like.

Cocoa was important in Mexico among the Aztecs, who, though they did not cultivate the tree, made a chocolate drink from the beans which they flavoured with vanilla and drank hot. Introduced from Mexico to the tropical regions of the Old World in the 17th century, cocoa is nowadays not only a universal delicacy but also a high-caloric and stimulating beverage (it contains caffeine the same as coffee and tea). Cocoa, as well as the chocolate made from it, are surprisingly enough used to flavour certain meat and fish dishes (mainly octopus). It is used in combination with onion, garlic and tomatoes, principally in Italy and Spain.

Though cacao is mostly propagated by seeds sown in nurseries, the best-quality cocoa can be obtained by the vegetative propagation (taking cuttings from the branches) of selected trees that produce the best seeds. In its way the cacao is a rarity in the plant world in that the flowers grow directly on the trunk (cauliflory) and older branches.

1

190

The small, oblong, cucumber-shaped fruits or pods (1) contain several rows of seeds or cacao beans (2). These are sweated (fermented), washed, dried and exported. The final stage of processing that gives us cocoa and cocoa butter is done industrially (involving hulling, roasting and grinding).

Nowadays cacao is raised chiefly in west Africa.

2

Garden Thyme
Thymus vulgaris

Lamiaceae

Garden thyme is becoming increasingly popular and more widely used. Whereas the Egyptians used it as a perfume and for embalming the dead and the ancient Greek scholar Dioscorides, an acknowledged authority even during the Middle Ages, stressed its medicinal properties (the plant's generic name is derived from the Greek 'thymos', meaning strong or manly), nowadays it is used primarily as a food flavouring.

Thyme may be used as a flavouring by itself, but usually it is one of the ingredients of proprietary herb mixtures. With parsley and bay leaf it serves as an ingredient of the traditional bouquet garni. Thyme is practically universal in its uses. It is added to soups, vegetables, fish, poultry and meats (particularly dishes prepared *au chasseur*), sausage meat, stuffings, salads, pickled gherkins and olives and is also used to make herb butter (often together with tarragon) and even to flavour honey.

Thyme is a sub-shrub up to 30 cm (1 ft) high, native to the Mediterranean region but nowadays grown in a variety of forms in many countries of Europe and in the USA.

It is best used fresh, for like most other culinary herbs it contains volatile oils, and for that reason it is commonly grown in the herb garden. Young plants, grown-on in spring from seeds, are bedded out when they are about 6 cm high. Thyme is most aromatic when it is beginning to flower and that is when it should be picked, dried and stored in air-tight containers for winter use.

The principal component of the volatile oil of thyme is thymol, which gives the herb its characteristic aroma and is responsible for its medicinal action. Thyme oil is a component of cough medicines and thymol is also added to toothpastes, mouthwashes and soaps, not only for its pleasant fragrance but also for its antiseptic properties.

Wild Thyme, Creeping Thyme
Thymus serpyllum

Wild thyme is unjustly considered a poor relation of garden thyme. It is less commonly cultivated and yet is widely distributed not only throughout Europe, but also in Asia, north Africa and North America, generally occurring in open, sunny situations and thus often found on loose, sandy anthills.

There are many varieties and forms, differing not only in the shape of the leaves and flowers but also in flavour and aroma, for example orange-scented and caraway-scented. Besides wild thyme *(T. serpyllum)* there are other species, grown more for decoration, that can be used as food flavouring, for example lemon thyme *(T. citriodorus)* which has a strong, lemon scent.

Wild thyme is harvested shortly before and throughout the flowering period by cutting-off the non-woody top parts. These are then dried in bunches hung in a well-ventilated spot, at a temperature not exceeding 35°C (95°F) like all plants containing volatile oil. Like garden thyme, wild thyme has a pleasant spicy aroma and slightly bitter taste. In cookery it is used the same as garden thyme.

Wild thyme is best distinguished from garden thyme by the flowers, which are stalked and arranged in dense panicles, whereas those of garden thyme are arranged in cymes. Wild thyme also flowers for a longer period than garden thyme and is thus excellent as a food source for bees. Garden thyme is a sub-shrub growing up to 30 cm (1 ft) high, whereas wild thyme is a creeping perennial herb (*serpyllum* is derived from the Greek word 'herpyllos', meaning creeping). Finally the main component of wild thyme oil is cymol, not thymol.

Fenugreek
Trigonella foenum-graecum

Fabaceae

Fenugreek is an annual herb growing up to 60 cm (2 ft) high and related to clover. It is valuable as a forage crop in the Mediterranean region. The exact translation of the botanical name 'triangular Greek hay' refers to the triangular appearance of the flowers and bears testimony to the fact that it was grown in the Mediterranean region as far back as antiquity. To this day it is found naturalized in Greece and Egypt and is also raised in Ethiopia, Lebanon, India, China and Argentina.

The hard, golden-brown seeds are used as a food flavouring. These are about 4 mm (1/4 in) long and are contained in long, slender, long-beaked pods, as many as 20 to a pod. Ground, ripe seeds have a penetrating and rather unpleasant scent and for this reason are never used by themselves but as an ingredient of pungent mixtures, mainly in certain kinds of curry-powder. In India the roasted seeds are used as a substitute for coffee.

The seeds germinate very rapidly and the seedlings may be used in winter to make a tasty and refreshing salad, the same as the seedlings of garden cress or mustard.

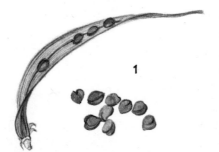

1

Fenugreek grows best in a sunny location in a well drained sandy soil with ample lime. The seeds (1) should be sown in spring directly in the ground where the plants are to grow and the seedlings thinned later on. The whole plants are harvested when about two-thirds of the pods are ripe and arranged in bunches to further ripen and dry. After this the seeds are hulled and dried.

The seeds contain up to 3% mucilages, which are used in the pharmaceutical industry and to give a finish to cloth in the textile industry.

197

Black Truffle
Tuber melanosporum

Truffles are fleshy, edible, potato-shaped ascomycetous fungi that grow underground. Most highly prized as delicacies and very expensive to buy are four species of the genus *Tuber;* namely *T. melanosporum* (1), the black truffle of Perigord, France, and the less aromatic. *T. aestivum* (2), *T. brumale,* and *T. magnatum. Choiromyces meandriformis* (3) and *Terfezia leonis* from the family Terfeziaceae are highly prized as well. The best quality seasoning is obtained from the black truffle which grows in the oak woods of southern France and northern Italy. Of all the edible truffles it is the most prized for its flavour. All truffles love warmth and grow in broad-leaved forests. *T. aestivum* is found fartherst north in Europe and may also be encountered in Switzerland and Bohemia. Because truffles grow as much as 30 cm (1 ft) below the ground, dogs are trained to scent them out. The mycelium is dug back into the ground in the area of their natural distribution to encourage their spread. The first truffles are formed four years later.

Truffles were a great delicacy in ancient Rome, where they were shipped in large quantities from north Africa. The Romans roasted them or cooked them in red wine and ate them with olive oil. They were also used to flavour pâtés and stuffings. In the Middle Ages they were believed to stimulate

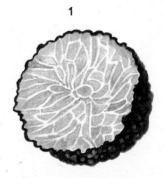

1

2

sensuality. In France they have been
commercially gathered since 1770. They
may be eaten by themselves roasted, stewed
or sautéed or used to flavour chicken, roast
goose liver, various roasted meats, salamis,
pâtés and as a stuffing for goose. They are
excellent for making a truffle ketchup.

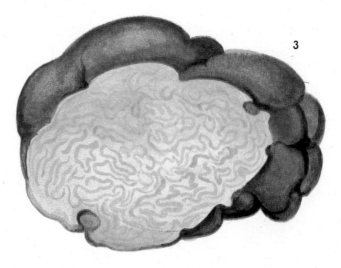

3

Stinging Nettle
Urtica dioica

Urticaceae

In rural areas chopped nettle is fed to goslings, it is also a popular component of shampoos, but people often forget that it is also a tasty and very wholesome vegetable and flavouring. This is due, perhaps, to the fact that nettle is a kind of cinderella amongst plants — unattractive, covered with stinging hairs and growing on waste ground and in ditches. However, do not be led astray by this. Though young spring shoots must be picked with gloved hands, when scalded they lose their sting and have a slightly bitter, spinach-like taste. Cooked alone like spinach or used to flavour spinach, nettle gives the dish a lovely green colour because its leaves contain a large amount of chlorophyll (the green pigment). They are also rich in Vitamin C, so important to one's health, particularly after the long winter. Chopped, scalded spring shoots or leaves may be used to flavour spring vegetable soups and vegetables served with meat. In some regions a baked mixture of eggs, breadcrumbs, chopped ham and chopped nettle is traditionally served at Easter time.

Nettle is a perennial and very stubborn weed growing up to 120 cm (4 ft) high, which spreads not only by means of seeds but also by its thick, creeping, branching rhizomes. It is dioecious, which means that the male and female flowers are borne on separate plants. Only freshly-picked nettle is used in cookery as it is not suitable for drying. For this reason it is a seasoning of early spring, when the fresh young shoots are available.

Vanilla
Vanilla planifolia

Orchidaceae

Vanilla is the only spice obtained from the aristocratic family of orchids. In the wild its twining stems climb high up into the tops of trees, anchoring themselves by means of aerial roots. The flowers are large and coloured pale green; each opens for a single day and can be pollinated by one kind of bee found only in Mexico. Thanks to this small bee, Mexico maintained its monopoly on the export of vanilla for 300 years up until the 19th century. It was known to the Aztecs, who used it to flavour cocoa long before the discovery of America by Europeans. Nowadays, it is raised not only in Mexico but elsewhere, chiefly in Madagascar, for it can be pollinated by artificial means. It is propagated by cuttings and trained up artificial supports or small trees. It begins to bear fruits in the third year. These are 16-to 30-cm-(6- to 12-in-) long pod-like capsules (known as vanilla pods) which are harvested while still immature so they do not burst. First of all they are scalded briefly with hot water and then submitted to the lengthy process of wilting and drying, during which they turn a dark colour and acquire their characteristic aroma. Good quality vanilla is supple and small crystals of fragrant vanillin are visible on the surface. Vanilla must be stored in an air-tight wrapper or container to preserve its aroma.

Vanilla is used solely for flavouring sweet dishes such as puddings, custards and chocolate dishes, cake fillings and ice cream. Vanilla essence, made from extracts of the pod, or vanilla sugar (castor sugar placed in a closed jar together with a vanilla pod thereby absorbing its aroma) are used as flavouring.

Nowadays, synthetically produced vanillin is often used instead of vanilla; it is cheaper and more convenient. The aroma of genuine vanilla, however, cannot be matched because it is the result of the natural balance of vanillin and small quantities of other aromatic components contained in the pods.

203

Grape Vine
Vitis vinifera

Vitaceae

The manufacture of wine as a beverage made from fermented grape juice antedates history. The first vintners were probably the ancient Armenians, who fermented the fruit of the wild grape vine way back in the early Stone Age (between the tenth and eighth millenium B.C.).

In Europe it was the Greeks who first cultivated the grape and introduced it in the 7th century B.C. to Italy and the territory that is now France. Its cultivation in America dates from the 16th century A.D.

Nowadays the principal wine-making countries are France, Italy, Spain, Portugal and Greece. And it is these nations that use wine to flavour their national dishes, chiefly roast poultry, meat and game. Even a small amount of white or red wine added to foods gives them an indefinable flavour imparted during cooking. In cooking the alcohol evaporates, but the delicious flavour remains, becoming mellower as cooking proceeds, and even confirmed teetotallers need have no fear of eating such food. White and red wine is also used to make wine vinegar by fermentation, during which the alcohol is changed into acetic acid. Such vinegar is finer than white table vinegar and particularly good in dressings for salads.

Dried, ripe grapes, available in shops in the form of raisins, sultanas and currants are also used as flavouring in cookery. Raisins are the dried fruit of a small dark seeded grape whereas sultanas and currants are seedless. They are added to sweet yeast dough to make buns and fruit breads, and cream-cheese fillings as well as to sweet sauces served with meat.

It is presumed that the original grape vine growing in the forests of Caucasia was a dioecious plant. The evolution of the present-day varieties traces its beginnings to the late Stone Age, when man learned to till land and began cultivating the grape vine. Long-term breeding and selection has produced a great many varieties differing not only in the colour, size and shape of the fruit, but also in flavour and aroma.

205

Ginger
Zingiber officinale

Ginger, with its tall leafy stems up to 1.2 m (4 ft) high, somewhat resembles a reed. The flower stems are about 25 cm (10 in) tall. The zygomorphic flowers have only one stamen, the other two being modified into a strikingly coloured lip. The pungently aromatic rootstock has been much in demand as a spice from the far distant past to the present day.

This perennial plant, native to tropical Asia, was known in ancient China and India and is referred to in Sanskrit as 'sringavere'. Ginger was shipped from its original home to southern Europe by Arabian merchants before the Christian era. It occurs frequently on the pages of the 3rd-century Roman cookbook *'De re coquinaria'* written by Apicius Caelius.

It is sold as fresh pieces of root, ground to a powder, candied, preserved in syrup and as an extract for making ginger ale. In home cookery ginger is most commonly used finely ground in cakes, pies and sweet dishes in general as well as in soups and with meats and fish. Ground ginger is also a basic ingredient of curry powder and is added also to ketchup. The greatest consumers are the Arab countries, England and the USA.

In England ginger has been a traditional spice since the 9th century, but Europeans were not acquainted with the plant itself until the late 13th century when it was described at almost the same time by both Marco Polo and Pagolotti. In the 16th century Francisco de Mendoza of Spain began cultivating ginger in Jamaica. Chief producers nowadays are Jamaica, southeast India, tropical west Africa and China.

Ginger is propagated by vegetative means, by cutting the rootstock into pieces and planting these out in light and moisture-retaining soil. It is harvested (ploughed up) 6 to 12 months later.

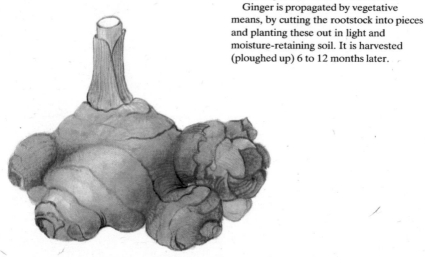

GROWING HERBS

In Europe people still use imported dried herbs and spices far more often than fresh herbs. This is perhaps due to the once prevalent convention that the extravagant use of pepper, saffron and other costly spices from the East is the mark of a lavish cuisine and a high-class upbringing. However, home-grown herbs can substitute some of those imported from the Orient. All you need is a small space in the garden about 2 m (6 ft) square, but even without a garden herbs can be grown in pots on the windowsill. The pleasure of raising your own herbs and the fascination of watching the plants grow and develop under your care, compensates many times over for the slight effort required. Man's natural atavism, his close bonds to the earth, make it possible for him to cast aside his daily cares and worries by working outdoors.

As herbs do not need to be grown in large quantities there is no need to have more than two or three plants of each species. The selection is wide and so the choice is up to you — choose what you want according to your own tastes and needs. Every collection, however, should include such herbs as chives, chervil, southernwood, tarragon, hyssop, lovage, marjoram, basil, oregano, thyme, parsley, savory and sage. However one can just as well grow all species of onion, celery, chamomile, wormwood, marigold, sweet pepper, caraway, costmary, coriander, rocket, fennel, lavender, garden cress, mint, watercress, nigella, poppy, purslane, radish, mustard or fenugreek.

There is naturally no universal rule for growing herbs. Each has its specific requirements and each thrives in different conditions. However most of the herbs listed above can be grown together in the small garden if provided with good garden soil and sufficient water, light and heat. The soil must provide the plants with all the necessary nutrients, it must be moisture retentive so the plants do not dry out but at the same time must be well aerated to permit oxygen to reach the roots. Sandy soils that lack humus and retain neither nutrients nor water are as unsuitable as heavy clay soils that have very poor drainage, retain large amounts of water and prevent the passage of air to the roots. Before planting, prepare the soil by adding humus in the form of leaf mould, rotted turves, well rotted manure or garden compost. The ideal soil is well drained but at the same time retains the necessary nutrients, well aerated and will neither pack down in wet weather nor form a crust when conditions are dry. The soil must also be deep enough to accommodate deep-rooting plants.

The quality of the soil can usually be improved, but light and heat depend on the geographical location. However, when planning the herb garden always choose a warm, sunny and sheltered place, so the plants are provided with conditions at least somewhat like those of their native habitat. They will reward you by growing well and developing flavour and aroma.

Every soil, even the best, deteriorates after a time for its fertility is depleted by the growth of the plants. Extra nutrients should therefore be provided every year or so by applying a proprietary balanced fertilizer. Take care not to overdo it, however, for generous feeding will lead to lush growth at the cost of development of flavour and aroma. One more thing — most herbs are lime-loving plants and if the soil is deficient in lime, this, too, should be added by digging it into the soil in the winter. Do not, however, apply lime and well-rotted manure or compost at the same time.

Most herbs are propagated from seed. In the case of annual and biennial herbs this is the only possible method. Seeds are usually sown in spring, after all danger of frost is past, either directly in the ground where they are to grow (the seedlings are then thinned to the required spacing) or in trays or pots. The plants can be sown in trays in early spring, and kept in a frame or greenhouse to protect the tender seedlings from night frosts. These are then planted out in their permanent positions when all danger of frost is over. Such plants grow more rapidly and are ready for use at least a month earlier.

Biennial herbs grown for their foliage or roots should be cultivated the same as annuals, for otherwise they will produce flowers early the following spring and die down as soon as the seeds are ripe. Perennial herbs can likewise be grown from seed, but they may also be propagated by vegetative means — by the division of bulbs (garlic, saffron) or splitting-up and replanting clumps of older plants. Older plants should be divided in spring or early summer so they have time to root properly before winter sets in. This revitalizes old plants which will then have more vigorous and healthy growth again for several years.

As the growing season draws to a close with the onset of autumn it must be kept in mind that practically all perennial herbs are natives of warm regions where frost is unknown (thyme, hyssop, sage, oregano, etc.). For this reason they should be cut back to about 10 cm (4 in) above the ground and in areas where frosts regularly occur, covered with a protective layer of dry leaves, straw or evergreen twigs for the winter. This should be carefully removed in spring when growth starts so that the plants are not attacked by fungus diseases which would flourish in the warm moist environment.

Hydroponics is gaining in popularity nowadays. This is the method of growing plants in a nutrient solution instead of soil, and is particularly suitable for growing house plants as it eliminates the need of daily watering. It can also be used successfully for growing many herbs. All that is needed is an opaque container of suitable size and shape and a mixture

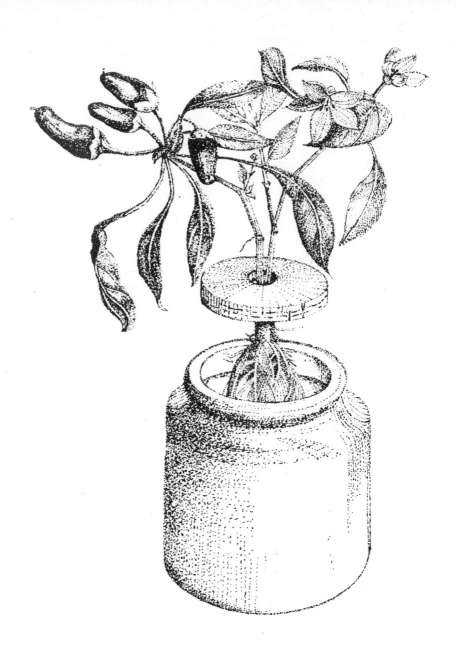

Soilless (hydroponic) cultivation of plants

of mineral salts, obtainable from most garden centres. There are complete kits available on the market, so try out which is best for the herb you want to grow.

HERBS AND HEALTH

Opponents of herbs and spices in cookery generally use the stereotyped argument that they are harmful to our health. The reply to this is simple: every excess is harmful to our health. Besides, many things that a healthy person can do are taboo for those who suffer from some disease or ailment. People with gall bladder trouble are advised not to eat fatty foods and diabetics must eliminate sugar from their diet. The same applies to the use of herbs. If you have an excessive secretion of gastric juices you should not use herbs that stimulate their flow. Similarly it is not advised to drink strong coffee or tea before going to bed for they stimulate the activity of the cerebral cortex, the heart, the vascular system and respiration. Wise and moderate use of herbs, however, acts as a medicine rather than a poison. Why just take a look into the past: at one time no difference was made between culinary and medicinal herbs and predecessor of our present-day herb garden is the medieval 'hortus sanitatis', or garden of health.

USING HERBS AND SPICES

Knowledge of the characteristics of aromatic substances is extremely useful to the modern cook. What happens to herbs and spices when they are added to food? In the preparation of cold dishes it is a simple matter, for there is no need to fear that the aroma will evaporate together with water during the cooking process. On the contrary, it is recommended to prepare cheese spreads, herb butter, salad dressings, cold sauces and the like at least an hour before serving so that the ingredients will blend thoroughly and the flavour will be at its peak.

Quite the opposite is true in the case of cooked foods. Here herbs are generally added shortly before the end of cooking (in the case of stewing, braising or roasting), particularly in the case of fatty foods, or just before the food is served. Exceptions to the rule are dishes made of minced meat, pâtés and stuffings where the herbs are thoroughly mixed with the other ingredients and thus protected by the mixture during cooking. Instead of the essential oils being carried off with the water vapour they dissolve in the fats present in the mixture.

These points should be kept in mind not only when using herbs but also when preserving and storing them. The commonest method of preserving herbs is by drying, apart from a few exceptions, to which attention is called in the text accompanying the colour plates of the individual species. There is no need to point out that even the most carefully dried herbs cannot compare with fresh herbs and so it is recommended to use fresh herbs whenever possible. Otherwise the general rule is that the more rapidly herbs are dried and the lower the temperature during the drying process the better their quality. If you wish to dry herbs at home spread them out in thin layers on rust-free, fine-mesh chicken wire or muslin-covered frames placed in a dry, well-ventilated place where the temperature does not rise above 30°C (86°F). Best-quality dried herbs are obtained by freeze-drying, which requires complex equipment and is a method that is being increasingly used commercially.

Dried herbs are stored either whole or only slightly crumbled in air-tight containers and crushed or powdered, when necessary, just before use. Even so, their quality gradually deteriorates and so it is recommended to dry only as much as is needed, a year's supply at the most.

An excellent method of preserving herbs, even though their use is then limited, is in the form of herb vinegars, which can be stored for an unlimited time.

HERB MIXTURES

Special shops offer not only individual herbs but also various mixtures. A list of the ingredients as well as instructions on how to use the mixture is generally printed on the packet. In recent years shops have been offering increasing numbers of these mixtures. In many instances, however, they are purely commercial merchandise often of poor quality, which instead of providing diversity to our fare generally has the opposite effect. True, it makes the cook's work easier but rules out the use of her creative talents. This, of course, does not mean that all herb mixtures should be tarred with the same brush. Many are mixtures with a long-standing history that have their established place in cookery to this day, regardless of commercial trends influenced by current fads.

Curry-powder is a classic example of such a tried and tested mixture. It is of Indian origin and in Tamil, the language spoken by people in southern India, the word 'kari' means sauce. Because there are many different versions of this sauce in the various parts of India the ingredients used in preparing curry powder also vary. The principal ingredients are pepper, chilli, coriander and turmeric; others may include cinnamon, ginger, cardamom, nutmeg and mace or allspice, fenugreek, cummin, mustard seed and poppy seed. All are finely ground and some have previously been lightly roasted. Indians themselves are not in the habit of using these ready-made mixtures. They prepare only a basic mixture consisting of lightly roasted coriander seeds, lightly roasted chilli and pepper and add whatever other ingredients they want as they cook, depending on the type of dish they are preparing.

Another ground mixture which is a basic ingredient in preparing Chinese and Vietnamese foods is the 'five spices mixture'. This is a very delicate blend of equal parts of Chinese pepper (the fruits of *Xanthoxylum piperitum*), star anise, Chinese cinnamon, cloves and fennel. In the Far East it is widely used for seasoning pork dishes.

Sauces and pastes are also herb mixtures, first and foremost of these being ketchup, which likewise originated in the Far East and was introduced to Europe in the late 17th century. Ketchup (ke-tsiap in Chinese) was originally the name for a salt solution used to pickle fish and for fermented fish extracts, whereas today it is applied to a wide variety of spicy salt extracts. In old cookbooks one will find many long-forgotten recipes for different kinds of ketchup. Nowadays there is no need to prepare and bottle it at home when there is such a wide range to choose

Pepper mill

from on the market. Two of the most popular are tomato ketchup (made of tomatoes flavoured with onion, salt, sugar and spices) and mushroom ketchup (made of meadow mushrooms that are similarly flavoured).

There should always be a bottle of ketchup on the dining table and along with it a bottle of Worcestershire sauce. Though it takes its name from the town of Worcester, in southwest England, it is of Indian origin, the recipe having been brought from Bengal to Worcester in 1837 by the British Governor. The governor ordered the sauce he was accustomed to using in India to be made up for him at his local pharmacy, but then he refused to take it because its taste did not begin to compare with that of the sample he had brought home with him. It lay completely forgotten in the cellar of the pharmacy for several years until one day the owners stumbled across it during a general clean-up and discovered, to their pleasant surprise, that it had acquired an excellent flavour. The sauce sold well and having luckily found the old recipe, they immediately set about making it on a larger scale. Its popularity spread rapidly, not only in Britain but throughout the world, and to this day Worcestershire sauce is still made according to the original recipe brought from India. The basic ingredients are vinegar, soy and molasses and an infusion of anchovies, chilli, ginger, shallots, garlic, plus about 20 other tropical fruits and spices. It is not boiled but prepared by maceration and lengthy ripening in large oak barrels as it was in the cellars of the Worcester pharmacy in the last century.

Another herb mixture is the very hot sauce or paste from Mexico called tabasco. It is made by cooking fresh chillis together with salt, vinegar, sugar, garlic and other spices. Similar pastes called chilli sambala ranging from mild to very hot are used in Indian cookery. Fresh chillis are also used to make a very tasty Indian chutney, consisting of a paste made of crushed chillis, coconut and dried coriander leaves plus salt and lemon juice.

One of the most popular herb mixtures, called 'bouquet garni' can be bought ready made up or prepared at home by each individual cook as she wants. It is prepared by tying together a sprig of thyme, three sprigs of parsley and a small bay leaf, plus whatever the housewife fancies, such as wild thyme, marjoram, lovage, celery leaves, a bit of mace, orange or lemon peel, cinnamon, sweet pepper or a garlic clove. Instead of tying the herbs together they may be put in a square of cheesecloth tied with a cotton, which makes it possible to use small herbs as well as sprigs. The bouquet garni is removed from the pot before serving.

Another widely used herb mixture which should be included in this account is the one known as 'fines herbes'. The principal ingredients are parsley, chives, rosemary and savory, plus others such as onion or garlic, pepper, mustard seed and nutmeg, depending on the manufacturer, but the mixture can also be made up by the housewife herself. It may be used in winter in place of bouquet garni.

A powdered herb mixture that is becoming increasingly popular in recent years is the 'barbecue' mix, used on roast and grilled meats. Its aroma is reminiscent of the smell of smoke from a wood fire and creates the illusion of meat cooked outdoors over an open fire. Ingredients include ground garlic, cloves, sweet pepper, chilli, salt, sugar and monosodium glutamate.

Many herb mixtures are made up for specific uses. Listed below are a few examples.

Herb Mixture	Ingredients
for pâtés	white pepper, cinnamon, ginger, bay leaf, mace
for gingerbread	cloves, cinnamon, star anise, ginger, cardamom, mace, allspice, orange peel, anise
for goulash	lots of sweet pepper, pepper, allspice or cloves, thyme, marjoram, caraway, turmeric, onion
for poultry	thyme, marjoram, rosemary, sage, savory, basil
for fish	bay leaf, white pepper, ginger, allspice, onion, coriander, chilli, mustard seed, dill sprigs, thyme
for pickling cucumbers	dill seeds or sprigs, bay leaf, allspice, pepper, cloves, mustard seeds, onion, horseradish, grape leaves
for grilling	sweet pepper, curry, chilli, pepper, thyme, oregano, salt
for sausages and salamis	pepper, allspice, cardamom, coriander, marjoram, thyme, mace and nutmeg, caraway, ginger, chilli
for game	thyme, oregano, allspice, bay leaf, pepper, sweet pepper, juniper berries
for ragout	sweet pepper, ginger, turmeric, coriander, mustard seeds, cardamom, caraway, pepper, allspice, nutmeg, cloves
for fruit (juices, compotes, marmalades)	cinnamon, cloves, ginger, star anise, cardamom

This list is intended to serve only as a rough guide pointing out the possibilities of various combinations. Often far simpler use is made of herbs in cooking with just a single herb, the end result being more subtle and delicate.

RECIPES FROM VARIOUS COUNTRIES

The evolution of the art of cookery did not follow the same course in all places. The distinctive dishes characteristic of the various nations are the result of many factors — geographical, climatic, political, and often religious, as well as specific local factors. They are distinctive not only in the selection of basic ingredients (meat, vegetables and side dishes) but also in the use of native herbs and spices. Thus, for example, typical of French cookery are ragouts and bouquet garni. In China meat cut in small pieces is cooked rapidly and served with a delicately seasoned sauce and white rice. Popular in the USSR are hearty, seasoned soups served with sour cream. India's highly spiced dishes are often unpalatable to the European.

The rapid development of foreign trade, tourist travel and the universal exchange of information after World War II brought with it the rapid spread of national dishes to all parts of the world, thus making cookery more and more international. Though world cookery is becoming more uniform this process is bringing greater diversity to the cookery of the individual regions.

The following selection of recipes from various parts of the world are traditional in their use of various herbs. They may bring a welcome variety to your menus, too.

Chicken Kung-pao   China

1 oven-ready roasting chicken
2 teaspoons cornflour
5 tablespoons oil
50 g/2 oz peanuts

1 teaspoon ground ginger
3 tablespoons soy sauce
2 dried chilli peppers, halved
salt

Skin and joint the chicken. Sprinkle the joints with cornflour. Heat the oil in a frying pan and sauté the joints until browned on all sides. Lower the heat and cook for a further 10—15 minutes, until the chicken is cooked through.

Add the remaining ingredients and cook, stirring, for 1—2 minutes. Serve hot, with boiled rice.

Beef Fillet with Cream Sauce   Czechoslovakia

675-g/1½-lb piece fillet of beef
50 g/2 oz salt pork strips
100 g/4 oz prepared mixed root vegetables
— parsley, celery, carrot and onion
5 peppercorns
3 whole allspice
1 bay leaf

½ teaspoon dried thyme
100 g/4 oz butter
strip of lemon peel
salt
300 ml/½ pint soured cream
25 g/1 oz plain flour
juice of ½ lemon

Lard the fillet of beef with the salt pork strips.

Place the prepared vegetables in a lightly-oiled casserole dish and add the peppercorns, allspice, bay leaf and thyme. Lay the meat on the vegetables and pour over the melted butter. Cover with cling film and leave in the refrigerator overnight.

The following day add the lemon peel and a sprinkling of salt. Roast in a hot oven (220°C, 425°F, Gas Mark 7) for 15 minutes. Add about 150 ml/¼ pint boiling stock or water and continue cooking, basting the meat occasionally, for a further 10–15 minutes, until the meat is cooked to your liking.

Lift the meat on to a board and cut into thin slices. Arrange on a serving plate, cover and keep warm.

Press the vegetables and liquid through a sieve, discarding the peppercorns, allspice and bay leaf (or blend in the liquidiser). Blend the soured cream with the flour and stir into the vegetables. Cook, stirring until the sauce thickens. Add the lemon juice. Serve the sauce in a sauce boat or poured over the meat.

Rabbit Gibelotte   France

25 g/1 oz butter
150 g/5 oz belly of pork, cubed
1 (1.5-kg/3½-lb) rabbit, jointed
2 tablespoons brandy
25 g/1 oz flour
200 ml/7 fl oz beef stock
200 ml/7 fl oz white wine

1 clove garlic crushed
1 bouquet garni
salt and freshly ground black pepper
12 small onions, peeled
225 g/8 oz button mushrooms, halved
croutons to serve

Melt the butter in a pan. Add the pork and cook over a gentle heat until the fat runs. Drain the pork and reserve. Add the rabbit joints and sauté until browned on all sides. Pour over the brandy and flame.

Stir the flour into the juices then stir in the stock and wine. Add the garlic, bouquet garni and seasoning. Bring to the boil, cover and simmer gently for 30 minutes. Add the fried pork, onions and mushrooms and simmer for a further 30 minutes, or until the onions are tender. Serve with croutons.

Christmas Pudding   Great Britain

225 g/8 oz plain flour
2 teaspoons mixed spice
½ teaspoon ground cinnamon
½ teaspoon grated nutmeg
175 g/6 oz fresh white breadcrumbs
225 g/8 oz shredded suet
225 g/8 oz dark soft brown sugar
225 g/8 oz raisins
225 g/8 oz sultanas

350 g/12 oz currants
100 g/4 oz chopped mixed peel
50 g/2 oz blanched almonds, chopped
225 g/8 oz cooking apples, peeled, cored and
* grated*
grated rind and juice of 1 lemon
2 eggs, well beaten
150 ml/¼ pint brown ale or beer
2 tablespoons brandy or sherry

Sift the flour and spices into a large bowl, add all the remaining dry ingredients and mix until thoroughly combined. Add the cooking apples and mix well. Beat all the remaining ingredients together and pour into the dry ingredients. Combine thoroughly and divide between two well greased 1-kg/2-lb pudding basins.

Smooth the top of the mixture with the back of a wet spoon and cover with greased greaseproof paper. Cover with a double layer of foil and seal, either with string or by twisting the edge of the foil against the rim of the basin. Steam over fast-boiling water for 5–6 hours, then leave until cool.

Remove the covering from the puddings, turn them out of the basins and wrap securely in clean greaseproof paper and more foil. Store in a cool, dry place.

To serve, steam for 2–3 hours and turn out onto a warm serving dish. Decorate with a sprig of holly.

Stifado   Greece

1 kg/2 lb boneless hare meat (alternatively use lean lamb or braising steak)	1/2 teaspoon ground coriander
	2 sticks cinnamon
800 g/1¾ lb tomatoes, peeled	salt and freshly ground black pepper
150 ml/¼ pint oil	1 unpeeled orange, cut down into
2 teaspoons vinegar	4 sections almost to the bottom
2 cloves garlic, crushed	1 kg/2 lb small onions, peeled
2 bay leaves	

Cut the meat into large pieces. Blend the tomatoes in a liquidiser to give a smooth puree. Alternatively, cook gently until reduced to a pulp, then rub through a nylon sieve.

Add the tomato puree together with all the remaining ingredients, except the onions, to the meat in a heavy-based saucepan and bring to the boil. Reduce the heat, cover the pan tightly and cook over a very gentle heat for 1 hour. Add the onions and cook gently for a further hour. Check the quantity of liquid frequently during the cooking time, adding a little water if the casserole becomes too dry. Remove the bay leaves and cinnamon.

Arrange on a warmed serving dish – the meat on one side, the onions on the other and the 'orange flower' in the centre. Serve with fresh bread rolls and a Greek white wine (e. g. Retsina).

Hungarian-Style Mushrooms   Hungary

2 green peppers	2 onions, minced
3 ripe tomatoes	1 tablespoon paprika
675 g/1½ lb mushrooms	salt and ground black pepper
juice of 1 lemon	1 teaspoon cornflour
50 g/2 oz butter	4 tablespoons soured cream

Pour boiling water over the peppers. Leave for 2 minutes, then peel, halve, seed and slice the flesh. Skin the tomatoes, chop and press through a nylon sieve or blend in the liquidiser. Remove the stalks from the mushrooms, slice the caps and sprinkle with lemon juice.

Heat the butter in a pan and saute the onion until softened. Add the mushrooms and sauté for a further 5 minutes. Add the peppers, sprinkle with paprika and cook for a further 5 minutes. Sprinkle with salt and pepper and stir in the tomato puree. Cook for a further 3 minutes.

Mix together the cornflour and soured cream and stir into the mushroom mixture. Reheat, but not allowing the mixture to boil. Serve hot.

Stewed Beef Masala   India

1 tablespoon coriander	2 teaspoons ground turmeric
1/2 teaspoon ground caraway seeds	1/4 teaspoon chilli powder
1/2 teaspoon ground ginger	1 tablespoon shredded coconut

218

malt vinegar
2 tablespoons oil
1 onion, sliced
2 cloves garlic, crushed
2 green chilli peppers, chopped

6 slices fresh root ginger
450 g/1 lb chuck steak, cubed
salt
stock or water

Mix together the coriander, caraway seeds, ground ginger, turmeric, chilli powder and coconut. Add sufficient vinegar to make a smooth paste.

Heat the oil in a pan and sauté the onion, garlic, chilli peppers and root ginger for about 5 minutes. Mix in the coriander mixture and the meat, stirring so that the pieces of meat are coated with the mixture. Season with salt and add sufficient stock or water just to cover the meat. Cover and simmer for 1½–2 hours, adding more liquid if necessary. Check the seasoning and serve.

Prawns and Rice (Nasi goreng) — Indonesia

3 tablespoons oil
3 cloves garlic, crushed
2 medium onions, peeled and chopped
salt and freshly ground black pepper
1 teaspoon chilli powder
1 tablespoon soy sauce

450 g/1 lb freshly cooked long-grain rice
100 g/4 oz shrimps or prawns
100 g/4 oz cooked chicken or veal cut into
  cubes
½ cucumber, sliced
1 thin omelette freshly made

Heat the oil in a saucepan, add the garlic and onion and saute until soft but not browned. Season lightly. Stir in the chilli powder, soy sauce and cooked rice. Cook over a gentle heat, tossing the rice continuously, until heated through.

Place in a warmed serving dish and top with prawns or shrimps, chicken meat and cucumber slices. Garnish with strips of omelette and serve with a tomato or pepper salad.

Neapolitan Pizza — Italy

15 g/½ oz fresh yeast
300 ml/½ pint lukewarm water
450 g/1 lb flour
1 teaspoon salt
5 tablespoons oil
salt and freshly ground black pepper

450 g/1 lb ripe tomatoes, peeled and reduced
to a puree
1 clove garlic, crushed
12 anchovy fillets
100 g/4 oz black olives
fresh chopped or dried oregano

Cream the yeast with a little of the water then cover and leave in a warm place until frothy. Sift the flour and salt into a bowl, add the yeast liquid and remaining water. Mix to a soft dough together with 2 tablespoons of the oil. Knead on a well-floured surface until smooth and elastic. Place in an oiled bowl, cover with a damp cloth and leave in a warm place until doubled in size (about 2 hours).

Re-knead dough to remove all the bubbles and divide in two. Roll out to make two large pizzas of approximately 0.5-1-cm/¼-½-inch thickness. Place on greased baking trays and brush with some of the oil. Mix the tomato puree with the garlic and season lightly. Spread over the pizzas, leaving a border of dough. Arrange the anchovies and olives on top and sprinkle liberally with oregano. Drizzle the remaining oil over the top.

Bake in a moderately hot oven (200°C, 400°F, Gas Mark 6) for approximately 40 minutes until the edges are golden. Serve hot.

Chicken with Chocolate Sauce   Mexico

1 (1.5-kg/3¹/₂-lb) oven-ready roasting
   chicken
salt
225 g/8 oz white bread, cubed
3 tablespoons milk
100 g/4 oz butter, melted
2 eggs
100 g/4 oz frankfurters, chopped

3 cloves garlic, crushed
1 teaspoon ground sage
freshly ground black pepper
¹/₂ teaspoon chilli powder
2 onions, peeled and chopped
1 tablespoon cocoa powder
200 ml/7 fl oz white wine
250 ml/8 fl oz single cream

Rinse the chicken, pat dry with absorbent kitchen paper and sprinkle lightly with salt. Mix together the bread, milk, half the butter, the eggs and frankfurters. Add one clove of garlic, a pinch of sage and season with pepper. Mix together well and use to stuff the bird.

Place the stuffed bird in a roasting tin and brush with the remaining butter. Sprinkle with the chilli powder and remaining garlic then place the onions in the tin and cook in a moderately hot oven (190°C, 375°F, Gas Mark 5) for approximately 1¹/₂ hours, until cooked through but not dried out.

Remove the chicken to a warmed serving dish and keep hot. Spoon out any excess fat, then stir the cocoa into the pan, add the wine and bring to the boil. Simmer for a few minutes then add the cream and reheat thoroughly, but do not boil.

Carve the chicken and arrange on the serving dish with a little of the sauce. Serve the remaining sauce separately in a warmed sauce boat.

Dill Sauce   Sweden

50 g/2 oz butter
50 g/2 oz flour
1 litre/1³/₄ pints beef stock
6 tablespoons chopped fresh dill
2 tablespoons wine vinegar

2 tablespoons sugar
salt
2 egg yolks
a few sprigs of dill to serve

Melt the butter in a saucepan, add the flour and cook over a gentle heat, stirring continuously, until a pale golden brown. Gradually stir in the stock and bring to the boil. Simmer for a few minutes until thickened. Add the dill, vinegar and sugar and season with salt.

Stir the egg yolks with a little of the sauce then return to the saucepan and stir over a gentle heat for a few minutes. Do not allow the sauce to boil or it will curdle.

Serve in a warmed sauce boat. Garnish with a few sprigs of dill and serve with boiled beef, minced beef patties or any poached or baked fish.

Solyanka of Mixed Meats   USSR

450 g/1 lb chuck steak, cut into cubes
50 g/2 oz butter
1 onion, peeled and finely chopped
2 tablespoons tomato puree
3 large gherkins, halved lengthwise and
   sliced
1 tablespoon capers
50 g/2 oz stuffed olives

2 bay leaves
350 g/12 oz mixed cooked meats, cut into
   cubes (optional)
To serve:
150 ml/¹/₄ pint soured cream
chopped fresh dill or parsley
slices of lemon

Cover the beef with slightly salted water and simmer until tender. Meanwhile, melt the butter in a saucepan, add the onion and cook until soft but not browned. Add the tomato puree, cooked beef, mixed meats and cooking liquid. Stir in the gherkins, capers, olives, bay leaves and mixed meats. Bring to the boil, reduce the heat and simmer for 10 minutes.

Serve in warmed individual dishes topped with soured cream and garnished with chopped herbs and slices of lemon.

INDEX